The Modeling Handbook

The Complete Guide to Breaking Into Local, Regional & International Modeling

EVE MATHESON

$15.95

Peter Glenn Publications
Publishers since 1956
42 West 38th Street, Suite 802
New York, NY 10018
212.869.2020 / Fax: 212.354.4099
www.peterglennpublications.com

ISBN: 087314-300-0
4th Edition-1999

Cover Credits:
Photographer: Russell Adair
Models: Rebecca Farrare, Pat Patterson
Cover Designed by Dale Stebbins/Stebbins Advertising

Designed by Chip Brill/CB & Associates

Printed in the United States by Choice Catalog
1040 First Avenue, New York, NY 10022

Dedicated with love to my family

Table of Contents

Table of Contents

A Note of Thanks

My sincere thanks to all of the model agents and industry experts who took time out of very busy schedules to answer questions and supply information. Without their encouragement and support I could not have written this book.

Foreword

The ever-changing world of modeling is becoming an increasingly major force in the world of show business, attracting thousands of young hopefuls who seem to get younger every year. The million dollar contracts, product endorsements, future acting and singing careers all require a business knowledge, which the average 14 to 16-year-old doesn't have. The pursuit of these contracts requires a very strong will, perseverance and guidance. It also comes with a lot of rejection, jealousy and pressure from colleagues. THE MODELING HANDBOOK is a must for the new model, male or female, and for the parents. It will provide them with everything there is to know about the modeling industry.

When I began modeling, over twelve years ago, there were limited resources to help me get started. I experienced several unnecessary disappointments and received wrong information. I had to rely on my intuition and morals to succeed.

I shall never forget my introduction to the modeling world, via a modeling competition in New York. I was a nervous, inexperienced wreck. Although I won the runway competition and was whisked off to live in New York from Washington D.C., to be with a top agency, I only wish I had had access to THE MODELING HANDBOOK then. I would have been more secure and made wiser decisions during my first year in the business.

Eve Matheson attended my first competition. I'll never forget her kind yet concerned face. I have since modeled throughout Europe, as well as New York, for every major designer, and at several shows. I still see her taking notes, asking questions, getting expert advice and following the modeling movement. Believe me, this book is not something Eve has written just sitting at home by the fireplace. She has hands on experience and information from top international agencies, top casting directors and top models including her daughter Tracy and is generous enough to pass it on. I am proud to know Eve, not only as a familiar, kind face in a crowd, but as a pillar of information to the modeling industry.

Just how does one get started? Where are the most lucrative markets? What should one expect from the business in the first year? How does one make the transition from modeling to acting? All the answers to these questions and many more are included in this exciting, informative new book.

Future models take advantage of the opportunity to be one step ahead of the game, by reading THE MODELING HANDBOOK thoroughly and carefully, again and again. It is certainly the groundwork to super stardom.

Shailah Edmonds

Introduction

I have been involved with the modeling profession for over 20 years (perish the thought!). While I never pursued it as a full-time career, our daughter Tracy did, modeling in New York, London, Paris, Milan, Portugal and Scandinavia before going to medical school. When Tracy first went to Europe, there was no information available on how to break into the modeling profession, let alone be successful in it.

At the end of her first year, she was well aware of the obstacles and problems facing fledgling male and female models. As a parent and journalist, I felt impelled to investigate and find answers. I wanted to talk to as many reliable sources as possible to collect detailed information and advice which I could pass on. I did not want anyone to be in our predicament.

Tracy's input helped immensely. I traveled to the fashion capitals of the world and interviewed models, agents, photographers, casting directors, make-up artists, stylists, parents, school directors and many others associated with the modeling industry,

When I first started traveling and doing research for this book, my focus on the young girl who wanted to become a model. I discovered, however, that there were other categories of models which needed to be explored and explained. I found that an increasing number of men were interested in a modeling career. Many had already become very successful. I expanded my vision and talked to some of these established international models as well as agents handling male models in the worldwide markets. They provided excellent advice on how to get started and how to enjoy a lucrative career.

As we know from movies starring supermodels Kim Basinger (an Oscar winner!), Elle Macpherson, Cindy Crawford, Lauren Hutton, Sharon Stone and others, modeling and acting careers overlap, especially if we also take into consideration the billion dollar television and commercial industries. Research in this area provided indispensable advice for models and actors.

Then came another dimension – the child model and actor. Parents plied me with questions on how they could get their children started in the business. Children and parents require very specific information and counseling. I interviewed the very best agents and casting directors for children in the world. They gave me honest, accurate details. Advice and warnings poured in and my original focus for this book expanded yet again.

With anorexia disorders on the rise in this country, I was relieved to find that industry experts, from agents and casting directors to clients, felt a responsibility to deal with this crisis. I am glad to report that the waif is now out and a healthy look is in again.

I am also happy to report that the Plus size (size 10 and over) is going strong and encompasses quite a wide age span. A young girl who is healthy and happy at size 10, 12 and 14 and over is slowly beginning to realize that she is beautiful because of - not in spite of - her size.

In every chapter of this book, there is information crucial to a successful career. There are specific answers to a myriad of questions.

Modeling is a fabulous profession, but it can be a brutal business. I don't want to inflate or shatter dreams. My aim is to educate the hundreds of young men and women who pursue modeling careers every year. I also want to explain the business to parents and family members whose concern and involvement can be major contributions to success.

Chapter 1

What Does It Take To Be A Model?

You are tall, slim, have beautiful cheekbones and a drop dead smile. Your family and friends say you should be a model. You are convinced you could strut down a runway in Paris or Milan and look just as fabulous as any supermodel, given the right make-up, clothes and a little practice. It looks so easy. Believe me, it isn't! The supermodels have paid their dues. They know about grueling schedules, disillusionment, disappointment and rejection. They would be willing to discuss this downside of the business with anyone who is interested, but the media hypes the glamour and the world is only interested in their fame, exotic lifestyles and considerable fortunes.

The traditional classic beauty is no longer the only type who will succeed. She will always be sought after, but today's model must be unique. She must not only be attractive and have a great personality but trendy with the ability to change her look.

Youth, stamina, good features, a well-toned body, patience and great attitude are all essential to success. That is just the beginning. To work on the international circuit, a girl must be at least 5'9" tall, with 34-24-34 statistics. A boy should be 6', wear a 40 Regular jacket and be aged twenty-one or over. Ideally, a girl should be sixteen and a high school graduate. Obviously there are exceptions to the rule. We have all seen very young models in the fashion magazines. supermodels like Lauren Hutton, Linda Evangelista, Christy Brinkley and Carol Alt have broken the age barrier at the other end of the scale and proved that a model's career can far exceed the average five-year age span.

Why is it so necessary to have so many attributes? A great attitude and the ability to take criticism and follow direction means that you will be an asset on an assignment and save the model makers time and money. Supermodels are made, not born. It doesn't happen overnight. It can take two years to establish a successful international career. Patience must be one of your virtues. Self-confidence will help you withstand rejection on a daily basis. This is not easy for anyone, especially a vulnerable teenager alone in a foreign city. Family support is an invaluable confidence booster. Travel across time zones means jet lag and this combined with long hours of hard work demands stamina. Stamina demands sufficient sleep and good nutrition. Good eating habits and exercise must be part of the agenda.

Every year the competition becomes stronger as hundreds and thousands of young men and women pursue the same dream. Realizing this and knowing what it takes to be even a little better than the next model will give you an advantage. Professionalism is a major component to success. This means being punctual, considerate, prepared and reliable. An easy smile, great disposition and a super personality are great assets.

Modeling is a billion-dollar business. There is no room for mediocrity. You must be extraordinary. Above all, you must be emotionally and mentally prepared and absolutely ready to make the commitment.

If you are not tall or thin enough to be an international fashion model, remember that this is only one aspect of the business. Other categories, which do not have stringent height and weight requirements, are discussed in this book. A good example is catalog modeling which can be very lucrative. These days the modeling and acting professions overlap and their scope is large. Somewhere there is a niche for almost everyone.

If modeling is your dream, pursue it. I am by nature very optimistic. I truly believe that by realizing the downside of a situation one is motivated to acquire the skills and knowledge required to make a dream come true.

Modeling is a great career. It is glamorous, exciting, fun and the financial rewards are enormous. While it doesn't last forever, it opens doors for other opportunities. Enjoy it while you can and make plans for the future.

If you have read this chapter and absorbed the information you probably know if you have what it takes to be a model. The next step is to learn how to break into the business and make the dream come true.

Chapter
2

How Can I Become a Model?

There is no written-in-stone way to start a modeling career. There are, however, definite guidelines. To be successful you must have an agent whether you work on a local, regional or national level. He or she will be your 'mother agent' and will find work for you, guide your career and decide on the appropriate agent when you go to the foreign fashion capitals. All agents are constantly searching for new talent.

How do you find an agent? There are a number of different approaches. A lot depends on your age, height, where you live and the type of model category that fits your look. It is important that you find the right agent, one you feel you can trust and talk to as a friend. First of all, if you are sixteen or seventeen years old, 5'9" tall, weigh 120 pounds, have good cheekbones, a beautiful complexion and long slender legs, you have an excellent chance of being accepted by a top agent in a major market. New York, Chicago, Dallas, Miami and Los Angeles are considered major markets. Ask a friend or relative to take a couple of snapshots or Polaroids. One should be a headshot showing your face and hair, the other a body shot showing your legs. If you have a bathing-suit picture you can use that, too. Every agent emphasizes that at this stage you should not spend large sums of money on professional pictures. They do not like posed pictures or portraits. They want to see you looking relaxed and natural. If they are interested in you, they will arrange photographic sessions. The best source for names and addresses of legitimate agencies is the International

Directory of Model and Talent Agencies and Schools, published by Peter Glenn Publications, New York. Tel. 212-869-2020. Call the agent and ask if they have open calls, a time set aside each week to see new faces. Take your pictures in at the appointed time. If you plan to visit several agencies you will obviously need several copies. Put your name, address and telephone number on the back of each photograph. A good agent will know within seconds if you have potential and the decision to accept you will be made rapidly. If there are too many girls at the open calls to be seen individually, you will be asked to leave the photographs and you will be contacted later.

If you don't live near a major market, mail your pictures to the agencies and include a stamped, self-addressed envelope and a letter requesting an interview, the return of your pictures and the agent's comments. Generally you will receive a reply along the lines of: "We'd love to see you..." or "You are not our type..." When an interview is granted you will have to pay any travel or hotel expenses you incur.

If you fulfill the ideal model's requirements but don't feel confident or mature enough to live and work in a major market, or you are under 5'9" and therefore could not work in such an area at this stage, the best plan here is to start out at a local level. Seattle, San Francisco, Atlanta, Phoenix and Miami are good regional markets. Follow exactly the same procedure for the open calls or send a letter requesting an interview.

On the local level, call the agencies to ask if you might send pictures. If they agree, send them off and follow up with a telephone call a few days later. If you are concerned about the reputation of an agency, check it out with the Better Business Bureau, the chamber of commerce, or the industrial commission of the state in which you live. You can also check credentials with the closest offices of the Screen Actors Guild (SAG) or the American Federation of Television and Radio Artists (AFTRA). These are the two main unions for actors and models. You might have to write or call the head offices for the nearest branch: SAG, 5757 Wilshire Blvd., Los Angeles, CA 90036-3600, Tel. (213 549-6400); AFTRA, 260 Madison Avenue –7th Floor, New York, NY 10016, Tel. (212) 532-0800.

Be wary of MODELS WANTED advertisements in your local paper. and never arrange to meet or go anywhere with an agent, scout or photographer who stops you in the street. Accept his or her business card and investigate thoroughly.

If you do not have a model agency in your area I suggest you call on the fashion coordinators or buyers of your local department stores, or owners of boutiques and ask if you might model in upcoming fashion shows. Write to the fashion editor of your local newspaper or magazine and offer to model for a fashion feature. Call on reputable photographers in your area and ask if they could use you for commercial work. The old saying 'Bloom where you are planted' is good advice for some people. If you can work locally as a model or actor, make money and be fulfilled, you have one formula for success.

There are many thirteen to fifteen-year-olds who want to be models but have to finish high school. Often top agents who have found girls in this category will work with them and their parents in preparation of a career launch in Europe later on. It is an excellent time to lay the groundwork for an exciting future. If you are really interested in becoming a model, read as many magazines as possible and learn all you can about the modeling profession. To gain confidence take part in school, church, or local fashion shows. A teen modeling or self-improvement course at a department store would be a wise investment. Videos explaining runway techniques or special makeup skills for on-camera work are also good investments. If you have a weight problem, now is the time to overcome it permanently by developing good eating habits and exercising regularly. Stay away from drugs and alcohol. If you develop a dependency on any of these, modeling is out of the question. Smoking is also a health hazard.

Sometimes a model scout will approach a young man or woman in the street, mall or in a restaurant. This brief encounter can lead to an interview with a top agent.

Men who want to be models should know that they are in a female-dominated profession. There is no equality of the sexes in pay or job opportunities. The big consolation is that a man's career lasts much longer. He can work from the age of nineteen to forty-five or over. Height requirements for men are 6'0" to 6'2", jacket size 40 Regular or Long, waist 31-32, sleeve 33-35, neck $15\frac{1}{2}$-$16\frac{1}{2}$.

The approach for getting started is the same as for girls. Send snapshots and a letter to the all-male agencies or agencies with divisions for men. Be assured that Americans are the most popular male models in the world.

We have explored the different age levels and categories and the direct approach to starting a career. Here are some other approaches worth consideration. A model competition or a model search, if legitimate, can open up excellent career opportunities, as the following success story will illustrate:

Top model Beverly Peele was twelve years old and 5'9" when she won a local modeling contest in California, her home state. The prize was a scholarship to a modeling school. The school entered her in another contest, where Beverly won prize money and an opportunity to attend the International Model and Talent Association Convention in Los Angeles. Beverly was an immediate success; she was signed by a Los Angeles agency and worked in New York and Milan where she modeled the Collections. A year later she appeared on the cover of *Mademoiselle*. What a way to start a career!

Modeling conventions are another way of being discovered and signed by major modeling and commercial and acting agencies. The International Model and Talent Association Convention is an excellent example. This outstanding event is held in Los Angeles and New York and has launched many careers in the modeling or acting professions. There are many conventions held all over this country and Canada where contestants are seen by top casting directors and some of the most prestigious agents in the world. The chapter on competitions and conventions will help you evaluate these events.

A modeling school course, while not essential to a career in modeling can be of great value. I have seen this value increase in importance over the last few years as competition in the various markets has reached staggering proportions. If it is run by experienced professionals who are, or have been, associated with the modeling profession, it can provide a rewarding introduction into the business and lead to a lucrative career.

When you visit a school, study the curriculum carefully. Make sure it covers essential aspects of your prospective career such as runway technique, hair and makeup instruction, wardrobe, photographic posing, television commercial workshops, acting classes and in-depth discussions of the industry. Ask questions such as: Is the school licensed by the state department of education? Is it bonded? Does it have an agency and, if so, is that agency bonded and licensed? If it does not have an agency, does it have an affiliation with one? What are its connections with the major agencies around the country? Is it involved with a modeling association? What are the school's graduates doing – have some of them gone on to successful modeling careers? What are the present students doing? Are they modeling in the best fashion shows in town?

I spoke to a number of experts who shared their thoughts on modeling schools. Christiev Carothers was an international model, a school owner and a model scout before going into the Christian music business as a creative director in Memphis. She said: "I went to a modeling school course years ago and it changed my life forever. I learned so much. Unfortunately these courses always seem to have a scam stigma attached to them. The problems start when schools promise students they will be stars. Everyone who goes to school will encounter more and gain more. That's a guarantee. But very few will go on to be models—I won't even say stars!"

Canadian agent Alecia Bell, who has been in the business for many years, told me: "There are a lot of scams that take advantage of young girls. I have seen girls who have spent a thousand dollars on a portfolio but are too short to work. There are some fabulous schools that are very up-to-date and their instructors are trained to the ultimate. If a school has a very up-to-date curriculum and good teachers - that's super. But super girls are often taught bad habits and outdated techniques and it is a nightmare to have to retrain them."

Eileen Green, who owned an agency in Hamburg, Germany for many years, told me: "A modeling school course is important for any young girl because she will learn deportment and self-confidence. Even if she never enters the modeling world, it is not money wasted. It can help her with any career. But I do think that every school should have at least one lecture telling prospective models how to survive in Europe."

Jack Rasnic, founder and coordinator of the Models of the South convention, said: "Modeling schools have become better educated in ascertaining skills that major agencies require of their models. Everyone has discovered that a professional model cannot be just a pretty face; she must have skills in photography and acting as well as runway."

Barbizon International Inc., the modeling school conglomerate, is concerned about the future of young people and their education. Senior Vice President Thomas (Tom) Blungiardo told me: "Education is the process by which mankind watches a generation. Challenges have never been greater. A college education is no longer an elective, it is required.." In support of this philosophy, the Barbizon Corporation awards an annual $100,000 college tuition scholarship to the modeling school graduate they deem most worthy. Congratulations to Barbizon for giving back to the community.

Whether you find an agent by yourself or through the help of a modeling school, or a model search, competition or convention, the interview which will follow can make or break a career. This applies to an interview with an agency, a magazine editor, photographer, or other client. Your attitude is very important. You must be pleasant, positive and alert. Turn nervousness into energy. If the agent or client is having a twinge of doubt, a nice personality will weight the decision in your favor. Answer questions honestly and ask as many as you need. Shake hands at the beginning and at the end. Treat this experience as if it were any other job interview or college admission interview. Wear very little makeup and avoid bizarre hairdos! Wear an outfit you have worn before and in which you feel comfortable—you must look and feel great. Don't wear layers of clothing. Wear a dress, or skirt and blouse, that will show your figure and legs.

Acquiring an agent is not the ultimate guarantee of a successful career. A mother I spoke to at a modeling convention was overjoyed when a top agent accepted her daughter. She was quite amazed when told that this important step was not a guarantee of a successful career. However, top agents have a very good idea who will work and be successful. If you are accepted you stand a good chance of enjoying a great career.

These guidelines will help you get started. Believe in yourself! Don't be afraid to try! Keep your dreams alive!

Chapter 3

Explanation of Modeling Terms

To help you understand this book more clearly, here are some of the terms used in the modeling profession.

Book or Portfolio
This contains the photographs and tear sheets that show a client examples of your work.

Booking
A confirmed job assignment.

Casting
A casting is an interview for a film or television commercial.

Callback
This is a second audition for a job.

Composite, Card, Index Card (in England), or Sed Card
The above terms all mean the same. The Sed Card is named after its inventor, Sebastian Sed of the former Parker-Sed Agency in Germany. It is a group of pictures on one card showing a model in different poses and with different expressions. The card lists height, weight and measurements and the name and telephone number of the model's agency. It is a very important tool and should only be put together with the help of a legitimate, knowledgeable and experienced agent.

Dresser

This is the person who will help you change into various outfits with lightning speed backstage at a fashion show. Don't scream, slap, or swear at the dresser! You couldn't do the job without her.

Foreign Terms

Haute Couture is French for High Fashion. Prêt à Porter means Ready to Wear.

Translation of terms on composites:

	Italian	**German**	**French**
Height	Alttezza	GroBe	Hauture
Bust	Seno	Oberweite	Poitrine
Waist	Vita	Taille	Taille
Hips	Fianchi	Hüfte	Hanches
Size	Taglia	Konfektion	Ceinture or Taille
Shoes	Scarpe	Schuhe	Chaussures
Hair	Capelli	Haare	Cheveux
Eyes	Occhi	Augen	Yeux

Go-Sees

A go-see is a job interview with a photographer or a client.

Head Shot

A close-up photograph of a model's head and face.

Headsheet

An agency will usually have a book containing pictures and statistics of all of their models and/or a headsheet, which is a large sheet of paper containing the same details. This information is mailed to clients and is very instrumental in obtaining work. You will have to pay to be included in headsheets.

Loupe

This is a magnifying glass used to view slides and film.

Mother Agent

The mother agent is the name given to the agent who handles the model and successfully introduces him or her to the international scene.

On Location

This is where the shoot takes place. It can be a place you know well or an exotic spot on the other side of the world. This is your opportunity to travel, with all expenses paid including your salary.

Open Call (Or Open Interview)

A specific time set aside by an agency for bookers to see potential new talent.

Option

This is the term used when a model's assignment is put on hold because weather conditions are questionable or because the final decision to book him or her has not yet been made.

Photogenic

The ability to photograph well. No matter how great you look in person an agent or scout will always want to see your photographs.

Scout

Just as universities have scouts for football, baseball and volleyball talent, so model agencies have scouts seeking new faces around the world. Be very careful if you are approached by anyone calling him or herself a scout. Have an adult check their credibility. While in Paris, our daughter Tracy was approached by an alleged scout for the fashion house of Courrèges. I was suspicious of the man and Tracy and I went to Courrèges to check him out. I gave them a full description but it did not fit any of their scouts. When they saw Tracy, however, they asked her to model in their Fall collection. Some stories do not end quite so happily.

Shoot

Time spent in a studio or on location with a photographer or camera crew for an assignment.

Tear Sheets

These are pages from magazines and other publication that show a model at work. Since tear sheets indicate experience they are essential credentials.

Testing

Testing is the term used for a photographic session to produce pictures for a portfolio and composite.

Voucher

A voucher is a payment form and a contract between you and the client. It is essential that you fill these out correctly. The procedure is that you give a copy to the client, retain a copy and give a third copy to your agency immediately so that billing can be done without delay. (Never allow a photographer or client to add any conditions to the voucher or delete any reference to reproduction rights. And never sign a paper relinquishing reproduction rights without the approval of your agency.)

Terms Describing the Main Types of Modeling
Live Modeling
This refers to runway, showroom, fitting and trade show work. Runway models are fashion models who work at local, regional and international levels. The most exciting runway work is done at the haute couture (high fashion) designer shows in New York, Paris, Milan and London. Models must be at least 5'9" tall and have a 34" hip measurement and great stamina. In showrooms, models wear manufacturers' clothing for buyers of department and chain stores. A trade show model will represent a client's product at a trade show.

Photographic Modeling
This has two categories. The first is editorial, or print, which is excellent for prestige, your portfolio and your ego! The pay is not very good, however, with the day rate ranging from $120 to $400 for a magazine cover. The big payoff comes from the exposure, which attracts advertising or commercial clients. In the second category, commercial print, a model is photographed to sell a product.

Television Commercials
This is an extremely well paid category in this country and the United Kingdom but not in Europe. In the United States it has made modeling the billion-dollar industry it is today.

Catalog Modeling
As the name implies, this is for the production of catalogs. It is steady work and pays well. Hamburg, Germany, Melbourne, Australia, Miami, Chicago and Dallas are very big markets. Movie star Nick Nolte started out as a catalog model.

Specialty Modeling
This refers to such specialties as plus and petite sizes and handicapped, fit and parts modeling. The market for children is huge and merits special attention. I have devoted specific chapters to these categories.

Chapter 4

How Can I Be Successful?

I am convinced that education is the key to success.

The first thing you should do is read books and research the business. I feel strongly that lack of knowledge and false information are the main reasons so many young men and women fail in this career. Parents must also educate themselves. Many push their children into modeling careers. The pressure experienced by some young models in Europe from parents - especially mothers - is appalling. Understanding how the business works, what to expect and what is expected of you, is a major key to a successful career. If you are fortunate enough to be accepted by a major agency and sent overseas, jump for joy and then get down to the business of learning the highs and lows of a modeling career.

For the young model overseas, here are the problems and suggested solutions:

Homesickness

Homesickness is the first problem, but it is quickly overcome.

You will be so busy moving into your new home, meeting clients and photographers and posing for test sessions, that at the end of the day you will be too tired to think of being homesick. The answer is to throw yourself into your new career and make friends with other new models as quickly as possible. You can have a great time exploring the city and taking side trips on weekends. Don't be embarrassed by the fact that you are homesick. This is a very natural condition. However, it has crushed promising new careers time and time again. Understand it, accept it and deal with it!

Culture Shock

In the beginning, this is the biggest and most serious problem. A model must adapt to new customs, fashions, food, lifestyles, languages, currencies and transportation—and all at the same time.

One is forced to adapt quickly. Worrying about these changes will affect your looks, attitude and performance. A good solution is to read as much as possible in advance about the country where you will be working. You can also rent a video, which is an exciting way to see and learn.

Another solution is to spend time with a foreign-exchange teller at a bank in order to learn the currency of the country. Find German, French and Italian groups in your hometown and ask them to tell you about their country and its customs.(People are always pleased to brag about their country.) Study foreign-language magazines. When you arrive in Europe talk to models—especially those from your own country—and listen to their explanations of why life is different. Talk to your booker and agent. They are always delighted when models show an interest in something other than modeling. And above all, don't criticize local people and customs—at least not in public. Their ways may not be yours, but that does not make them wrong.

American friendliness, which as a foreigner I find charming, is sometimes misunderstood in Europe. Europeans are more reserved (with the possible exception of people in ski lines!). The delightful American eagerness to make friends is often misinterpreted as pushiness. You must be polite, courteous and quiet in restaurants and public places. You will be accepted graciously if you try to blend into that society and respect the customs. Good manners are important no matter what nationality you are or what country you are in.

Learning to deal with culture shock is an education. You will become more confident and independent. Within the first month, you will have broadened your outlook and expanded your knowledge.

Language Barriers

It is overwhelming to arrive in a country and not know a word of the language. You cannot make a telephone call or order a meal. Radio and television sound like gibberish and by the end of the day you are totally exhausted, not just from climbing thousands of stairs (elevators are unheard of in the older buildings in Europe) but from being constantly surrounded by foreign words and sounds. Trying to find your way around town can be most distressing.

Let me give you an example of my personal experience. When I was in Hamburg, my daughter Tracy wanted me to understand how difficult and frightening it is for a young model to find her way to assignments in a foreign city where she does not understand the language or the transportation system and cannot afford the luxury of taxis. To enable me to appreciate all of this, Tracy set up six hypothetical go-sees in various parts of Hamburg. She established a time limit and insisted I use only bus or subway transportation. I pleaded with her to accompany me but she refused, explaining (smugly) that as she knew how to get to these destinations it would defeat the object of the exercise if she came. I was haunted by her final words: "I will know if you cheat and take a taxi!" It was a frightening experience. I did not do well, to say the least. Within fifteen minutes, I had broken the law. I had leaped onto a train (which was going in the wrong direction) without a ticket and I was lost! The next few hours were a nightmare. I arrived (late) for two of the fictitious go-sees, bungled all attempts to reach other destinations and arrived back at the hotel (by taxi!) in a crumpled heap. A gleeful Tracy opened the taxi door with a loud "Tsk-Tsk!" and "Now, wasn't that easy? I can't wait until we get to Milan—you don't speak Italian either!"

One solution is to buy a beginner's foreign-language tape for your destination country. Play it constantly. Listen to it while you fall asleep and when you are on the plane. You will be amazed at how many phrases you will pick up. Your ear will become accustomed to the sounds. A phrase book comes with each cassette. Keep it with you. Learn a few words each day. This will be a great help.

Tear Sheets

First of all, avoid the misconception that in Europe it is easy to get tear sheets and make money quickly. This is quite wrong. It is an established fact that European clients are insisting more and more on booking experienced models who already have tear sheets. Consequently, it has become increasingly hard for a new model to work. In many cases, European tear sheets are needed in order to work in Europe. It is a vicious cycle.

It is also discouraging to discover that a tear sheet that brings you work in Switzerland will be taken out of your book in Milan because it is unsuitable for that market. So when you are told, in essence, that Europe is that "big tear sheet in the sky", don't believe it. Know that it will take time and money to get tear sheets that are good enough for your portfolio. Be prepared for this and be patient. Don't get discouraged—they will come eventually. Another point, however, is that even when you have done a job that will produce tear sheets, it will be some time before these are available to you. Fashion magazines are shot months ahead of publication and by the time they are on the market you may well have moved on to another country. Ask your booker, another model, or a friend to keep an eye out for them and send them to you. It is frustrating to have worked and to have nothing to show for it. Clients are not interested in explanations; they want to see evidence of work.

Money

Some models starve and live in appalling conditions because they don't have enough money. Many fall prey to bad situations because they don't have enough money. How much money is enough?

Apart from Japan, where the business is run quite differently (I have explained all of this in the chapter on Tokyo), a model should have sufficient funds to support him or herself for the first three months. An American, for instance, should take at least $1,500 to $2,000 to Europe plus a return ticket or additional funds for it. Insufficient money is a big problem and leads to other problems. But I warn you, do not travel with cash. Use travelers checks and, if possible, have at least one credit card. (A young photographer who arrived in Milan had his passport stolen en route and $2,400 in cash stolen within hours of his arrival in the city. He had to return to the United States.)

Why do you need this amount of money? First of all, it will take two or three weeks, probably even longer, to put together a composite or have pictures taken that are good enough to take on go-sees. (At this point, do not rush out for a session with a hometown photographer who doesn't know the European market. The photographer will make money and you will be left with useless prints.) A good idea is to find some current foreign magazines that will show you what "look" is in, in the various fashion capitals. A few photographs of this type would be a help to you and your European agent. Remember that a couple of good pictures are worth a dozen mediocre ones. Unfortunately the bad ones are always remembered. You will need money for food, for rent (even if an agent advances money, it has to be paid back—nothing is free!); for transportation and for many incidentals.

Unprofessional Behavior

Throughout this book agents, successful models and photographers stress the importance of professional behavior. What exactly does this mean?

First, let me give you an example of unprofessional behavior and its consequences. A young English model on a rapid rise to fame in Europe became conceited, overconfident and careless. She knew she was much in demand and thought clients and her agent would tolerate her less than professional attitude. She arrived late for work on several occasions. One day she didn't show up at all. A furious client called her agent, who in turn called the model's apartment. A boyfriend answered and told the agent that the girl had been working so much(!) she was tired and had decided not to go to work. The agent told the boyfriend to tell the girlfriend to come to the agency to pick up all her belongings. By the time the stunned model arrived her magazine covers, which had adorned the walls, had already been replaced by another beautiful face. No amount of tears would change the agent's mind. The agency's reputation was on the line. The model was finished.

Professional behavior means being reliable, punctual, adaptable, considerate, pleasant and loyal to your agent. And here are a few other pointers for fledgling models. A go-see is not an opportunity for a gossip session with other models while you are waiting to see a client. This time should be spent concentrating on what you are going to say and do when your turn comes. Don't ask to see another model's portfolio and don't show yours to anyone but the client. Your book is your business.

When you meet the client, smile, shake hands, introduce yourself and give the name of your agency. If you are nervous, transform your jitters into energy and enthusiasm. Don't ever apologize for a weak portfolio! If it isn't as good as it might be, spark the client's interest with your attitude and personality. Learn from successful models. Superstar Carol Alt attributes much of her phenomenal success to her professionalism. She told me: "There are many girls out there far better looking than I but you will never find one who is more professional." Follow Carol's advice. Be professional. Eliminate unprofessional behavior before it becomes a habit that will ruin your career.

Coping with the Unexpected

Sometimes actions speak louder than words.

I was at a fashion show recently when a model lost one of her shoes on the runway. She reached down, took off the other shoe and continued without missing a beat. Remember this tip, if this should ever happen to you!

Airline Tickets

Take the time to shop around for your overseas airline ticket. Your agent will advance money for your fare, but if you can pay for it yourself it is better.

You will eventually have to reimburse your agent; therefore, the cheaper the ticket the better off you will be. A word of warning. Make sure the airline is reputable and not likely to go out of business while you are in Europe. You could be left with a useless return ticket. Leave the return date open.

Here is another important point. Some large cities have more than one airport, so make sure connecting flights are from the same airport. Making a frantic dash from one airport to another is expensive and takes a lot of time.

I speak from experience. The day my daughter and I left for Europe I discovered that the airline we had planned to use had gone out of business. I had been in China until three days before our departure and had not heard of the airline's problems. Fast work by a travel agent secured two seats on a flight to London's Heathrow Airport. On the plane, I realized that our Paris flight departed from Gatwick. It would have been impossible to make the connection on time had my family not met us at Heathrow and rushed us through to Gatwick. We arrived in the nick of time, made the connection and met the agency representative in Paris as planned. It was a nerve-racking experience. It would have created a major problem for a young model and a distressing start to a career. So make sure you are booked on a reputable airline and that your flights arrive and leave from the same airport.

Overweight

Being overweight is not just another problem; it is a disaster! Don't go overseas hoping to lose a few extra pounds en route or within a few days of arrival.

Lose weight before you go. You will be weighed and measured on the first day at your new agency. Believe me, they will not be happy if you are overweight. It will hold up your progress, because a reputable agent will not lie about your weight on a composite. In Europe, they talk in centimeters. There are 2.54 of these little horrors to every inch. A few centimeters too many will mean that you won't work in fashion or catalog. As every agent told me, the bottom line is that models have to fit into the clothes! A new model must have as much of the market available as possible.

To help avoid this overweight problem, here are some tips on weight control. Foods are made up of: a) carbohydrates (2.4 calories per gram), b) proteins (2.4 calories per gram) and c) fats (4.8 calories per gram). Fats have twice the calories per gram and must therefore be watched and reduced in the diet. There are 3,500 calories in a pound of body weight. To control weight you must understand the intake and output of these calories. Well, we all know about intake! Output means exercise. You lose as many calories walking as you do running one mile; it just takes longer to walk. Your weight in pounds, multiplied by two-thirds, is the number of calories lost by running or walking a mile. To calculate the basic number of calories required to sustain your body weight when you are not exercising, multiply your present weight by 12 if you are a man (e.g. a 150-pound male requires 1,800 calories per day); and multiply by 11 if you are a woman (e.g. a 124-pound woman requires 1,364 calories per day). So, it is really quite easy to lose a pound a week, or even more, by reducing caloric intake and exercising. You will need an accurate list of calories contained in various foods. This can be obtained from a doctor, dietician, or reliable literature. Extra pounds mean tension, worry, depression, more eating, more weight gain and so on. Don't let it happen to you.

Excess Luggage

Still on the problem of weight but a different kind, let's take a look at the problem of excess baggage. It is expensive to fly with luggage that is overweight and it is an unnecessary expense to have to store it. Also, it is a nuisance to have at your destination.

Remember, hand luggage is not the excess that will not fit into your suitcase. I met one young model who had problems with both types of weight. She had paid $200 for excess baggage across the Atlantic and a further $200 on a rowing machine, in a vain attempt to lose the weight since signing the contract with her agent. What a disaster!

Rejection and Depression

These two problems seem to go hand in hand. From the moment you become a model you must face the fact that no matter how pretty or handsome you are, or how perfect your measurements, you are going to be rejected over and over again by clients and photographers.

It happens all the time—even to people at the top. It is part of the business. You must learn to live with it. It helps if you understand that the reason you do not get a particular job is not personal; it is because you are not the right type of look for that particular job. It also helps if you know that you will work eventually. Be determined not to get depressed. I remember sitting in one agency in Paris, waiting for an interview, when a gorgeous model came back from a go-see and announced to the world—and her agent—"Well, they absolutely hated me there. What's next?" With a brilliant smile she took the details of her next go-see and breezed out. That model had the right attitude.

She was positive. She was rolling with the punches.

Modeling is no place for the emotionally insecure. And don't forget: when the chips are down, you can always turn to the Super Agent. The power of prayer is amazing.

Insurance

The problem of accident and hospital costs can be avoided by having insurance before you leave home.

This is imperative! In some countries, you will be covered by insurance after you have worked for a while. Find out the details of this from your foreign agent. To be on the safe side, take out health and accident insurance for the first three months.

Inadequate Business Knowledge

Insufficient knowledge of the modeling profession and the situation abroad can be a big problem. Far too many young men and women believe that because a foreign agent has accepted them, their dreams of becoming a successful international model are soon to be realized.

This is a reasonable assumption, but it doesn't happen that easily. When a foreign agent agrees to take you overseas, it means that he or she believes that you have what it takes to model in that country, but there are no guarantees. That agent will work for you because that is the way he or she makes a living. This can take time.

Do not go overseas unless you have an agent at home who understands the overseas business and will keep track of your progress. A good agent will know exactly how you should be treated and how your career should be handled. Make sure that your school director and your parents ask the questions that need to be answered. Parents must know exactly what their sons and daughters are getting into. They should know about accommodations, commissions and finances. All agents have a list of rules and regulations concerning their agencies and policies. Ask for the details.

Excessive Drinking

Excessive drinking is a problem, especially in Germany, which is the first port of call for many new models and where the legal drinking age is fifteen.

Wild parties and undisciplined behavior result in models being dropped by the agency and even sent home.

Drugs

Drugs are highly prevalent everywhere today. To be caught with drugs means imprisonment and deportation. A model messing with drugs eventually loses everything.

Agents will not tolerate the unreliability and substandard appearance that ensues. An American agent warned: "A model may get away with using cocaine for two months, or possibly a year, but it always catches up."

The Playboy Scene

A girl who is well balanced, has a strong sense of self-esteem and has been well informed by her mother agent will not have a problem in this area. There are some very handsome men in Paris and Milan with gorgeous accents who like to surround themselves with beautiful girls.

The parties, limousines, furs and gifts are enticing, but the price is too high. When a stranger phones and invites you to a party, say no the first time and the second time and then you will probably be left alone. Modeling is a serious business. Late-night parties and drugs will affect your appearance and cost you your career, your self-respect and possibly your life. You don't need to do these things to be a successful model. Australian super model Rachel Hunter summed it up beautifully: "Real models don't spend their nights partying it away in nightclubs, hanging out with playboys and taking drugs. We are hardworking girls who usually start at 6 a.m.and have to be fit and alert because of all the traveling that is involved."

Stress

Stress is a model's enemy. It diminishes sparkle and self-esteem.

I have seen many young people lose jobs because tension and pressure made them appear inexperienced or lacking in personality. Don't be a victim of stressful situations. Build your confidence. Listen to compliments and constructive comments from people who are guiding your career. You will soon learn to recognize what is genuine. Dwell on the good remarks. Think only positive thoughts. Always treat other people as you yourself would like to be treated. If a booker or agent is hostile give him or her the benefit of the doubt. They are probably stressed to the limit at that moment. Respond with kindness and understanding. A smile always helps. Next time around some of your pleasantness will probably have rubbed off on them.

Here are some exercises to help ward off tension. Try to do them twice a day even when you are not being stalked by doom. First, learn this breathing exercise: take several long, slow, deep breaths, saying to yourself the word R-E-L-A-X. Think R-E while breathing in and L-A-X while breathing out. Now, start at the toes, work through the body and work upwards, relaxing these muscle groups: Breathe in and out while tightening and loosening the toes, the calves, the thighs and the buttocks. Exhale and relax. Breathe and push your stomach out. Exhale and relax. Now do the chest, arms, shoulders and neck area, crushing the arms to the ribs, tightening fists and hunching shoulders as you inhale. Exhale and relax. Finally, breathe in as you close the eyes tightly and tense the facial muscles. Exhale and relax. Take a few more deep breaths, remembering to repeat the word relax.... Now you are ready to pat yourself on the back and take on the world!

Finally, take heart. Even models at the peak of their careers have problems. One top model told me: "There is insecurity at the top. Most models have to worry about weight and we are always looking over our shoulders to see who the next superstar will be. But the biggest problem is that we tend to become totally turned inward and to think only of ourselves. It is important to be interested in other people and subjects outside of modeling."

Chapter 5

The Business

So far we have discussed the requirements for a modeling career, how to get into the business, the various types of modeling and terms used in the industry. Now it is time to learn more about the business and how it works.

What happens after you have been accepted by an agency? The answer, with slight variations, is the same for agencies worldwide. In the beginning you are considered a new face. The new faces division is like a small agency within an agency. First, there is orientation where you learn about the agency, its policy, contractual agreements, your portfolio, composite, testing and what is expected of you if you are to enjoy a good relationship with that agency. There will be an appointment with a hair stylist for a haircut (any resistance to change such as: "My boyfriend doesn't want me to cut my hair." will not be appreciated, as it could be an indication of how you will resist future changes.). Time will be spent deciding on your specific "look". The next important step is testing or photographic sessions. The more you test the better and more comfortable you become in front of the camera and the better the photographs for your portfolio. When you finally have the right photographs, you will be sent on 'go-sees' which means you will be sent to see clients, photographers and magazine editors. As they become interested and start to request you for assignments you will be moved to a working board. Sometimes, if you arrive at the agency in the beginning with a few good pictures, you will be sent on 'go-sees' immediately after which testing will begin.

And so the process of developing a modeling career is under way.

You will pay your agency a commission, usually 20 percent and you will be expected to repay the cost of airline tickets and money advanced for expenses. When you are working regularly, your average yearly income could range from $80,000 to $150,000. The earnings of super models soar into the millions.

I emphasize that to become an international model can take two years. This can be very frustrating, especially when, after a few months, friends will wonder why you are not on the cover of VOGUE, BAZAAR or ELLE. In this country, if you are under 18, a work permit obtainable through the board of education in the state where you will work is necessary. To obtain this, you will need your social security number, your birth certificate and a doctor's certificate stating that you are in good health. You must be 16 to work in Paris. Other countries will require visas and work permits but the agencies explain how these are obtained.

I cannot emphasize strongly enough how important it is to be educated about the modeling business before you get into it. There are certain cold hard facts that you must accept. When you become a model you become a product, a package, which must be marketed at the highest level by an agency and yourself. The modeling industry is in a constant state of flux. More and more agencies are opening, almost as fast as others are closing. Success waxes and wanes from one country to another depending on the economy, styles and trends. Career-makers, decision-makers, bookers and executives who have been ensconced with well-established agencies for years have bailed out to start their own agencies. The industry has embraced the technology of the Internet in order to save money and narrow the time and search for a model. State of the art high-tech equipment sends pictures from Milan to New York in seconds enabling composites to be changed every few days if necessary.

The excitement of the business continues to intensify, as does the competition. Today everyone is more informed. The business has become very international. If a girl is successful in New York, she is usually successful in London, Paris and Milan. American agencies look for girls who can leave their hometowns and compete in the worldwide market.

The modeling industry is getting more exposure and is expanding rapidly. This is partly due to the drama and excitement created by the fashion shows – 30 in Milan, 60 in Paris, 40 in New York, in one season. Hundreds and thousands of dollars are put into these productions which are covered globally by television. Celebrities and magazine editors from all over the world sit on the front rows giving the industry, and especially the models, incredible exposure.

As you can see, the excitement of a modeling career can reach dizzying heights. A young model must be informed and prepared. We are all probably the worst judges of our own talents. We need guidance and assessment. Listen to the advice of your agent, booker and other experts. Don't be embarrassed to ask questions. American agent Douglas Asch said: "I know about my business but I am ignorant about farming. That doesn't mean I'm stupid. Young people coming into this business have to learn a lot of new things. They have to be smart enough to learn and humble enough to say: "I don't know everything and I'm not going to do it my way." That's not easy to do. It takes a very fine balance. Mix that with a beautiful face, a good figure and a certain amount of sex appeal and you will have a girl who will be able to fit into the market pretty well."

I am constantly asked three specific questions: Should we take our child out of school for interviews and castings? Should we put college on hold? Why does a fashion model have to be a size 6 or 8? I'll deal with the school and college questions first as we were faced with these dilemmas when our daughter Tracy was in grade school and again when she was accepted by a European model agency at the same time that she was accepted for college. My advice is that if a great opportunity comes along which could finance college in the future and if your child is not going to miss important school work, then let her do it. Schools will work with you to make up for lost time. But if the child is upset and feels she will not be able to keep up at school if she takes this time out, or if she has to miss participating in a sports or social event which is important to her, then don't. As far as college is concerned, if a potential model with all the necessary criteria and a burning desire for this career is signed by a top agency, my advice is to put college on hold.

The answer to the third question concerning the obligatory size 6-8 for a high fashion or catalog model is that when designers make clothes they make one-of-a-kind. These are called samples and are always a size 6-8. The model must fit that size garment on a runway or on a fashion shoot.

Now here is a very important fact. If you come to a point when you decide that modeling, for whatever reason, is not for you, I strongly urge you to explore other aspects of the business. Model agents, bookers, makeup artists, photographers and so on can have fabulous careers. They are not necessarily easier fields to break into but height, weight and bone structure are not issues. And the challenge and excitement is there.

We all hear horror stories of abuse and scams in the modeling business. This is another reason why education for parents and fledgling models is imperative. I can assure you, however, that the good guys greatly outnumber the bad guys. I am a parent as are many of the agents, scouts, bookers and casting directors I have interviewed. We all have a great sense of responsibility to protect these young people.

Finally, I urge all up and coming models, male and female, to be patient, dedicated and informed. Helen Rogers, as the president of the International Model and Talent Association, said: "This is a 24-hour, seven-day a week job. Even when you are sleeping you are working on looking the part. You work at it for six days and on the seventh you should be praying for success the next week."

Remember that not everyone is cut out to be a super model. A recent survey revealed that out of the billions of women in the world, only a few dozen are considered supermodels!!! Today that statistic has multiplied but the number of megastars is still minute. One top New York agent is of the opinion that the super model era will end. He told me, "Times are tough. At the moment, clients will pay for a superstar but they don't want to pay for, or work with a model who is anything less. Consequently, designers do not want to create stars who can command astronomical fees. We will see more and more good models earning a lot less."

Chapter 6

Legal Matters

This invaluable advice on a model's legal rights comes from attorney, Colin C. Claxon of San Rafael, California, whose practice includes representation of models and agencies. Colin's wife, Lynn H. Claxon and their two children, Kristin and Scott own the very successful STARS, THE AGENCY, a full service model and talent agency located in San Francisco. His legal expertise and working knowledge of the modeling profession and agency business make him an authority on this subject. Here is what Colin has to say:

With all the glamour, glitter, excitement, energy and world travel, modeling is, for everyone in it, first a business; and everyone in it—the agent, booker, photographer, stylist, client and you—is in it for the money, usually lots of it!

The business world is run on contracts, commitments and definitions of what is expected and the world of modeling is no exception. You must have a basic understanding of what you can expect and what is expected of you; a mistake may be costly—for you.

The Agency Contract

Most agencies require you to sign a contract, usually exclusive: you agree that you will not model or accept a booking except through that agency and the agency agrees to locate bookings for you and expects to receive a commission from you, usually 20 percent of the amount billed. While most contracts appear to prohibit you from working for other agencies or switching during the contract term (usually one year), the contracts often provide for termination under certain circumstances, by either party or by mutual agreement.

You should think of such contracts as binding, because even though an agency may allow you to leave their agency and work elsewhere, they may demand that you continue to pay them for jobs which are on-going, or which are later renewed or extended. Too often young models wrongfully assume that these agreements are only moral commitments, when in fact they are binding and can be enforced. An agency that has invested time and money in building a model's look and book usually insists on protecting its investment. As an example, if an agency treats its models as exclusive and you accept a booking from another agent, or on your own, the agency can and will terminate you and you have breached a valuable confidence and harmed your reputation in what is really a small community worldwide.

Often agency contracts include (in the contract itself, or in an additional document), rules or guidelines setting forth what the agency expects from you, agency policies and specific procedures. These rules are binding on you. They may include such terms as repayment by you of expenses advanced by the agency for your development.

Read and understand everything that you are given and ask questions until you have all the answers. Agency contracts typically provide that the agency will bill the client for your services and receive the payment for you and permit them to cash your check pursuant to a power of attorney contained in the contract, even if the check is in your name. They will deduct their commission and pay the balance to you. This is standard procedure. Reputable agencies pay at least every two weeks if they have agreed to advance your payments, which means that they will pay you for your completed bookings before they are paid, which can take up to several months. Some agencies charge a model an administrative fee for advances to cover their additional costs in connection with the advances. The alternative is to wait until the agency is paid, commonly 30-120 days after the booking.

Your agency contract will usually provide that the agency can also deduct any monies advanced or loaned to you and all expenses paid on your behalf. Such expenses will include testing fees of photographers, film and print costs, long-distance phone calls made from the agency or the model's apartment, Federal Express or other special delivery charges (domestic or international), forwarding your book to other agencies, rent and living expenses and more. Be sure that you read your contract (or the accompanying rules and guidelines) carefully for the right of the agency to deduct such costs with or without your advance approval. Never be afraid to ask in advance which charges you may be expected to pay, because the practice varies from agency to agency. Always demand an accounting and explanation for all such deductions. The deductions should be itemized for you, usually on the check that you receive from the payment for your bookings.

The agency should not mark up or make a profit on such expenses; the deductions should represent the actual cost, nothing more. An exception is housing provided by agencies that typically may charge private apartment rent for a facility shared with many other models, as a way of allocating the cost. Your mother agency should be able to negotiate a maximum that will be charged to you for such a shared arrangement.

If your agency places you with an agency in another city (or a foreign country), your original agent is the "mother" agency. The mother agency holds your contract and remains in charge of your career development. The two agencies will be sharing commissions on your bookings, but the total agency commission you pay should not increase.

While you are working elsewhere, you should stay in touch with the mother agency. Never permit another agency to alter your appearance, i.e., cut your hair, without discussing that with your mother agency in advance. If you feel it is necessary to change agencies, do so only after consulting with your mother agency and obtaining their permission. Disagreements with the out-of-town agency should be referred to your mother agency. Taking care of you continues to be a part of their job.

A Word About Minors

If you are a minor, many states require that a court approves your contract with the agency or it will not be binding upon you! The law allows persons under 18 to repudiate (cancel) their contracts unless they have been approved in advance by a judge.

The agency will usually insist on court approval and will often prepare the required documents and arrange the court proceeding. You and your parents may have to appear before a judge to explain the arrangement with the agency. The procedure is quite simple. In order to protect you, as a minor, the court often requires that most of the money you earn be impounded in a bank until you are 18, but they do allow a reasonable sum for expenses and for your personal use. Once the court approves the contract, it is binding on you and your parents.

The Voucher

All agencies utilize some form of a multi-part voucher for each booking, for each model. Usually you will be given a book or package of blank vouchers. Be sure you read and understand each line and blank on the voucher form before you depart for your first booking. It is your responsibility to complete the voucher fully and correctly and if the information given to you on the set or at the shoot varies from what you understood when you accepted the job, call your agent from the shoot before you leave and clarify any doubts. (In fact, if any problem occurs on the set insist on stopping and calling your agent before proceeding with the shoot; that is the time to solve the problem.)

Never permit the client or photographer to alter the voucher in any way. Be sure that you obtain a signature on the voucher and that you return the correct copy to your agent. Your agent cannot bill the client (and you cannot be paid) until the voucher is turned in by you.

Most vouchers contain descriptions of the use that will be made of the pictures taken. Never permit a change to be made to that description. The use determines the rate and how much you are to be paid. Be certain that you know what the pictures will be used for. Never, never sign a blank model's or photo release under any circumstances. Use only the release given to you by your agent. A signed blank release allows the holder to use your pictures for any purpose, forever. Similarly, the client usually only has a limited time to use your picture: often only for one year. Usage beyond that period entitles you to more money.

If you ever see your picture on a bus, a billboard, packaging or hang tags, or in a magazine anywhere in the world, including Europe or Asia and feel that your voucher did not include such a use, or that the time had expired, contact your agency and report it, no matter how much time has passed. You may be entitled to additional compensation, including damages for unauthorized use. With the rapid expansion of the Internet and the ability to lift or morph pictures off the web, photo piracy has arrived. Unscrupulous photographers may sell your photos to a stock house (think of it as a large scrapbook) available on CD-ROM, or on-line and imagine what can happen. Your picture is your property and it must be protected and controlled—that is the job of your agency.

Model's Liability And Status

When your agent accepts a booking for you and you agree to do the shoot, a contract is created between you and the client. Models are independent contractors, not employees. If you are late or for some reason do not go to the booking without being excused by the client, the client will bill the agency for lost time on the set, which will include the time of the photographer, stylists, assistants and the other models. You are legally obligated for those costs.

Usually, the agency will deduct all such charges from your compensation on other jobs and such a provision is customarily found in the agency/model contract. As an independent contractor, you are liable for your own federal and state income taxes and the agency will not withhold them from your compensation. You will receive a 1099 Form at the end of the year.

You are responsible for filing and paying your own federal and state income taxes, including social security. You must keep track of all your expenses if you want to be able to deduct them.

An accountant can be very helpful in maximizing your deductions. After all, you are in business: the business of modeling.

Once you finish a job, or leave an agency, you are not entitled to receive unemployment compensation. Agencies do not carry workmen's compensation insurance or medical insurance for you. Unless you sign a personal services contract with a client for on-going work, you are not anyone's employee. You are an independent business person, in business for yourself.

A Regulated Industry

The modeling profession is a regulated industry in most states, certainly those in which most of the work is to be found (New York, California, Illinois and Florida for example). In those states, which have laws relating to the business of modeling, agencies are required to be licensed by the state and there are specific laws regarding the relationship and dealings between model and agency. Typically the state labor board or a similar department has jurisdiction over agency disputes.

Where such laws do exist they typically relate to forms of agency contracts, handling money in trustee accounts and may provide state arbitration of disputes. They may also prohibit certain unfair practices, such as insisting that a model use a particular photographer, requiring the purchase of a portfolio or pictures as a condition of accepting the model, or demanding that certain classes or training be taken. All such conditions are examples of fraudulent schemes.

Many reputable agencies hold open calls at no charge to the interested novice. This is an excellent way to find out whether you have the look they want. Avoid companies promising to find you representation if you will take a class or pay them a fee for their "help". The Better Business Bureau is a good source on information to check out such businesses. Often the Consumer Division of the local prosecutor's office has information on shady persons preying on would-be models.

Chapter 7

United States of America

I started interviewing people in New York for this book. Then I went around the world to interview agents in other fashion capitals. I returned to New York and talked to more agents, models, photographers and hair and makeup artists.

The pieces of the jigsaw finally came together here. Other American cities, however, merit attention because they offer excellent opportunities to models.

New York City

New York is the core of the modeling industry. Under the layers of glamour, expensive egos and jet-set life-styles there is enormous organization, dedication and incomparable savoir-faire. New Yorkers have a mental toughness often softened by hearts of gold. This takes some time to understand.

There are about fifty agencies in the city for men, women, children and parts models (models working specifically with eyes, lips, hands, legs, or other parts of the body). Every aspect of the industry is represented in this city. A top female model can make over $200,000 a year and this does not include the superstars who make millions. A good male model can make $50,000 to $75,000 a year. Women are required to be 5'9" to 5'11" with some exceptions and weight must be in proportion to height. The age range is sixteen to twenty-one and again there are exceptions at both ends of the scale. Many of today's superstars are over twenty-one.

Requirements for men are: height 6'0" to 6'2"; weight 165 to 170 pounds; measurements to fit a size 40 Regular or Long jacket, neck 15-15½, waist 30-32, shirt sleeve 33-35 and inseam 31"-34".

Agencies want experienced models with excellent portfolios, but they are always looking for new faces. Each agency has its own unique look. If you have it, they will take you on, test you and do everything in their power to make you a success.

New York is a fast-paced city, but at least everyone speaks the same language and there is an excellent inexpensive transportation system. This is a major plus for models who spend their days racing from one side of the city to the other. Being on the cover of American Vogue is every model's dream, but the chances of achieving it are remote. Remuneration for doing this, or any other cover assignment, is very small (between $200 and $400.) But once the word of a cover assignment reaches clients, photographers and other agents, the model is an immediate success. Her agency's phones will ring constantly. The financial rewards can be astronomical.

Most New York agents send their models overseas, mainly to Paris and Milan. Foreign agents respect their New York colleagues and are eager to keep this international alliance profitable and happy. When agents send their models to Europe they monitor their progress closely. The European agent strives for maximum exposure for the model, setting up appointments with photographers, editors and clients. The end result is a portfolio of pictures and tear sheets that are fairly sure to guarantee work and financial success in New York. The bonus is the wealth of experience the model has acquired in Europe. Today, with more magazines and more excellent photographers coming to New York, the opportunities for new models to acquire tear sheets here at home are slightly better.

The New York Collections take place in February and November and are a frenzy of excitement.

There is a super stratum of model agencies in this city as well as many others that are also excellent. They all have testing boards and take 20 percent commission. The organization that sets the rules and guidelines is the International Model Managers Association (IMMA). To belong to IMMA one must be established as a model manager, have a voucher system and a head sheet and have been in the business in New York for over a year.

Structured model agencies as we know them today began with John Robert Powers, a fascinating man, who after a brief spell as an actor and model, found himself spending more and more time acting as a liaison between photographers who needed models and friends of his—aspiring actors and actresses—who were only too delighted to pose in front of a camera. As the demand for models grew, Powers realized that there was money to be made by developing a model service. He also realized that there was a genuine need for a structured agency that would represent the models fairly. He made history.

In 1923, he started the world's first model agency in New York. Paulette Goddard, Barbara Stanwyck, Henry Fonda, Brian Donlevy and Gene Tierney were among his first models. The John Robert Powers Agency was an enormous success and dominated the business for over a quarter of a century. By the late forties, Powers had turned his talents to writing, cosmetics and a modeling school business. And another success story was beginning for a savvy young woman whose name was to become world famous—Eileen Ford.

The FORD agency has great prestige. In my travels, I found that the name Eileen Ford is known by people not even remotely connected with the business. Eileen and her husband, Jerry, have carved out the top notch in the history of the profession. They started their agency in 1947. It is a family operation with daughter Katie as the CEO. Katie worked in the agency's accounting department before opening the Ford agency in Paris in 1991 and other locations around the world.

Eileen pulled no punches when I asked her for her advice to new models. She said: "Too many parents want to live vicariously through their children. They are all too eager to send them over to Europe like sugarplum fairies. Avarice will get these people nowhere but into trouble. A child is a precious thing—to treat it like a commodity is cruel." She had this to say about young models going to Europe: "One fact you must face is that when a child is sent to Europe, she will receive no supervision. The super agents don't supervise—they don't have time. I am not talking about Switzerland or Germany. These countries are safe and someone like Soni Ekvall at Model Team in Hamburg will take care of her models. To go to Europe a child must be very well adjusted. They are subject to temptations, but these temptations are not handed out with a kiss and a gorgeous Italian accent."

Very young girls accepted by this agency are invited to live with the Ford family while they are learning the business. They make each girl feel loved and safe. Referring to the highly prevalent drug situation in New York, Katie Ford said: "There is a need to protect 16-year-olds from the world they are encountering today. I will run the agency in the same tradition as Eileen and Jerry. I am a parent and I will treat the models as my children. We will have the same family values." This agency is very diverse and represents every type of model.

Fran Rothchild and William (Bill) Weinberg are icons of the modeling industry. Fran co-founded the WILHELMINA AGENCY with the Dutch beauty Wilhelmina in 1967. The Wilhelmina Agency's namesake, Wilhelmina, had an extraordinarily successful career as a model. Her equally successful career as an agent ended when she died at the age of forty, a victim of lung cancer. When Wilhelmina died in 1980, Fran and Bill became joint owners. They are now retired from this agency. They were most generous with their advice and information on the industry.

Over the years Fran has seen thousands of models launch careers. Many have become superstars. We discussed the problems and misconceptions of new models. She told me: "So many girls have no idea what is involved in establishing a career. They think that when they come to New York or go to Europe they will be on the cover of Vogue in a few weeks. If you stop to think about it, Vogue has twelve issues a year. Of these twelve covers three or four may be reserved for major actresses and stars. This leaves seven or eight covers for all of the top models in the world. Newcomers must know and accept these facts. They should also know that there are girls who make a lot of money but have never been on the cover of a magazine. Above all it takes time to establish a career and make money."

Fran explained why it is necessary for new girls to go to Europe and why the European market is a significant factor in launching a career. "New models have to get tear sheets in order to put together a portfolio. The quickest way to do this is to go to Europe. There are many more opportunities there. Europe has more fashion magazines and many of these are published with greater frequency. New York shoots today for a magazine that will come out in a month or so. I do not think, however, that models should go to Europe unless a strong New York agent represents them. There are matters they can't handle by themselves."

Bill Weinberg expressed genuine concern for newcomers to the modeling profession both here and abroad. His answer to my question about advice for these young men and women was quick and serious: "Trust no one and be suspicious of everyone." He did not elaborate on this but his words haunted me as I traveled around the world and met young people who had been betrayed by "friends", or whose careers had floundered in the hands of unscrupulous agents.

The look at Wilhelmina is "clean, healthy, young." The age range is 14 to 50. There is a sophisticated division of older models. As baby boomers grow older there is an increasing demand for this type of model. There are fashion, print and runway divisions and also a very strong children's division. An agency spokesperson has this advice: "Parents must keep a very level head. This business looks so glamorous. If your son or daughter wants to model, inquire about a good agency. Don't get involved with schemes that involve thousands of dollars for pictures or schools. It's not smart to waste money on a portfolio when you don't know what anyone is looking for. These scams take your money, stop the reputable agents from finding the true talent we are looking for and give our business a bad name. Send a couple of pictures—snapshots are fine—to the top New York agents, or a reputable agent in your hometown. If they are interested, they will call you and take it from there. The industry is trying hard to make it very easy for people to inquire about this business in a legitimate way. The Ford, Elite and Wilhelmina agencies hold nationwide contests. This is a very cheap way to find out if you are the face that is being sought."

The COMPANY agency is a family-run, rapidly expanding business owned by Michael Flutie. The ratio of bookers to models is high, which means more attention can be given to individual careers. Michael told me: "When a girl makes a decision to come to an agency like Company, it is like making the decision to go to a small private university that has a low student enrollment, an excellent staff and excellent academic references versus a very large university with a huge staff and enrollment and an outstanding academic reputation. It is like choosing Vassar over Princeton or Yale. She won't get lost in the crowd and there will be a lot of motivation and supervision."

There are several divisions at Company including film and television divisions. The development division handles brand-new girls and models who have had up to two years of working experience. The management division is designed to manage careers of well-established models. "This is our superstar division. We have girls who work internationally and make a great deal of money. Our goal is to lay the foundation for a long, successful career in the development stage and then motivate and enable girls to move up into the management division."

Discussing age requirements Michael said: "We don't encourage anyone to move to New York full-time until they have finished high school. Education is a very important criterion with us. I don't think clients focus on how old a girl is as long as she is fresh looking, has good skin, is well-established and has a strong editorial book. I think a girl can work until she is thirty-five. However, it is too late to start a career at twenty-two." Michael reiterated the constantly recurring theme that a model should have a New York agent prior to going to Europe or any foreign country.

"I care very much about what happens to our youth, especially the people who enter this business. It is unfortunate that some of our young athletes and models fall into the hands of people pretending to be experts. Some people fail not because of their lack of ability but because of these people. A model should seek out the people in the business who have put strong emphasis on being honest and legitimate."

One agency owner gave me his views on recent changes in the industry: "These days fashion and commercial modeling overlap. We are also seeing older women in the business. Not long ago we booked a seventy-year-old for a cosmetic commercial. We had sent a fifty-year-old and were told she wasn't old enough. This would never have happened ten or fifteen years ago. The marketing people are beginning to realize that they have to make specific products for specific age groups and that teenagers are not the major money spenders in America." I asked him for his views on the multimillion-dollar contracts signed by top models. He said: "In twenty-five years we have come from a relatively small business to a multimillion-dollar industry. When someone is responsible for over three hundred million dollars worth of sales of a product, this is a very important spokesperson. We are looking at enormous amounts of sales tied to somebody's face and I think they are underpaid—which is a highly controversial position."

The ZOLI agency has been in existence for over twenty years. Rosmarie Chalem, who is Swiss, joined the agency in 1982. She had this advice for newcomers to the business: "If a young girl has the potential and a good head on her shoulders, this can be a very nice profession for her. From the very beginning she has to realize that it takes a long time to become a good model. It rarely happens overnight. When success does come she must not let it change her. We do send girls to Europe, but I warn them to be careful—especially in Milan. I only work with agents I can trust."

Girls must be at least 5'9" tall and be aged between fifteen and twenty for this agency. The men's division has about fifty models and has a strong worldwide reputation. Minimum height requirement is 6'0" and the age range is seventeen to fifty-five. The head of this division told me: "Men can enjoy a much longer career span. They have much more leeway. They don't have to be concerned with face wrinkles. In fact, we find that wrinkles give them more appeal. When they are photographed the lighting doesn't have to be perfect. If it is a bit shadowy or dark, it lends toward masculinity. Women have to have everything perfect. Men are lucky; they have very long careers. Our most prestigious models don't base themselves in one market; they make the circuit—Milan, Paris and London. It has become much more acceptable for a man to become a model. In Italy there are a lot of fashion magazines for men who study them and gear their style to that trend. Here, there are fewer magazines, but men are starting to read about fashion and to take a greater interest in what they wear. However, this is an industry where women make much more money than men. There are more fashion magazines and more products for women and women spend more money on all these things."

Owned by Frances Grill, the CLICK agency has been going strong since 1979. It has fashion, print and television divisions and represents men and women. Frances and her agency are very highly respected in the industry.

I love the name chosen by David Bonnouvrier for his agency—DNA, This stands for deoxyribonucleic acid, the molecule that makes up genetic material. "It's short and easy to remember," he explained, when I asked why he had chosen such a cerebral name. The rapid success of this agency is undoubtedly partly due to the input and expertise of David's father, Jerôme, who owned agencies in Paris for many years.

Camilla Cassels-Smith who helped start the agency told me: "Our true search is for the girl who will be high editorial, someone a particular photographer is going to be interested in. A girl may walk in and we'll say to ourselves, Steven Meisel or Bruce Weber would really like her. We then try to cultivate an image we can promote for her." Discussing the male model market she said: "There is no comparison to the women's market. There is less work and less money. However, there are some male models who make $500,000 annually." This agency is well connected internationally and the owners and staff are gracious.

John Casablancas, the dynamic force behind the ELITE agency, was born in New York of wealthy Spanish parents. He was educated in Switzerland and traveled extensively in Europe and South America. In 1971, after a trial-and-error period, he started his modeling empire in Paris with the opening of

Elite—an agency for the crème de la crème, the model superstars. L'Agence, an agency for grooming new talent, followed. In 1977 he fused his European savoir-vivre with his American savoir-faire and exploded onto the American scene. He opened an Elite agency in New York to the chagrin of his competitors. John Casablancas' rise to fame was rapid and his success phenomenal. He changed the face of the industry when he increased the rates of his models and they began to earn big money. Today he has the largest modeling network in the world. His "Look of the Year" model contest is the largest international model search. Elite is always looking for new models. Karen Lee, a not only beautiful but very caring, knowledgeable woman, is the director of scouting. Discussing the certain characteristics that people in the fashion industry look for, she said: "We look for a girl with a beautiful and interesting face that photographs very well. We look at lips, nose, the shape of the eyes, cheekbones. We also look for a long beautiful neck and long legs are important. The body must be in great shape. We look for girls who are 5'9" to 6'0" who wear a size 6 and/or 8. But as we all know there are exceptions to some of these rules. Kate Moss is 5'6"-5'7" and Gabrielle Reese is 6'3". Professionalism and a good personality are very important."

Started in February 1987, IMG Models is one of New York's leading agencies. It is a division of International Management Group, the sports management corporation that handles the commercial careers of the superstars of the sports world. Owned by Mark McCormack, IMG has produced an impressive crop of models that includes Julie Anderson, Carrie Johnson, Niki Taylor, Bridget Hall, Tyra Banks and Stephanie Seymour.

I spoke at length with Jeni Rose, the international director of talent and development, who is based in Paris. She told me: "I look for a face that I haven't seen before. I like a look that hasn't been done. I will follow a girl from the age of twelve until she is ready to come to New York at fourteen or sixteen. I like to make a rapport with the parents and the school director. I know that a girl who is twelve years old and 5'8" tall, or a girl who is twelve and 5'6" and wears a size 9 shoe, is going to grow taller. The difference between twelve and fourteen is just two years—four show seasons. If I start to have rapport now, I will have had two years of history with the parents and the modeling school by the time the girl is 14 and every other agency wants her." The men's division, which opened in 1998, was immediately popular and successful. IMG prides itself on precise, solid management and integrity.

In November of 1996, KARIN opened. This New York agency is a franchise of the famous Karin agency in Paris. Models from New York are sent to the agency in Paris, and also work through the Karin agency in Miami and vice versa. The philosophy of the agency is to give individual attention to the model and market the model individually. Director Scott Lipps said, "We like to keep a small, family style agency. Personalized attention is very important. We care about our girls." At Karin, they believe in "creating stars."

When asked about sending the models to Europe to get tear sheets, Scott said: "We definitely send our models to build up their books in Europe. New York is the hardest market. It is much better to already have a good book and work right away once you get to New York rather than trying to build your book in New York." Of course, there is always the exception!

This agency represents men, women and children. They also have a successful Plus-size division called CURVES. As a full-service agency, they really have it all!

McDONALD RICHARDS MODEL MANAGEMENT is one of the largest commercial print agencies in the world. Started by industry expert Arthur Bronfin in 1983, it represents adults of all ages and ethnic backgrounds. This agency's kids' and teens' division is great. With director Gary Bertalovitz at the helm, McDonald Richards has also opened a fashion division, MAC 2, which has gotten off to great start.

NEXT MANAGEMENT is one of the most innovative and fastest growing agencies. METROPOLITAN is a superstar agency in every sense. It opened in Paris in the mid-70's and in New York in 1990. NYTRO is exclusively for men. President Jan Gonet, who has had years of experience with the world's top agencies, discussed the male modeling business with me. He said: "It's in a state of flux. There are too many models and not enough jobs. Only the best are working. This is a very serious business. Men must be dedicated and behave in a professional manner. Looks, height and personality are important. For NYTRO, I look for someone who is strong and masculine; someone who can create an image and go beyond the obvious when they are in front of a camera."

PAULINE'S model management is a delightful agency, which was opened in August 1984 by Canadian-born Pauline Bernatchez, a former Paris model.

The name Heinz Vollenweider is known and respected from coast to coast and all over the world. Heinz, who is Austrian, owns IMAGES MANAGEMENT and MAXX MEN, which represent female and male models, respectively.

The fashion world logged on to Q MODEL MANAGEMENT, an exciting, state-of-the-art agency, when it debuted in New York in April, 1998. Q ushered in a new era of independent model management with a 21st century approach to an old philosophy: personal, one-on-one management. Q plans on maintaining the lowest model to agent ratio in the industry. They are very focused on the quality of the agency as an environment for all their models and bookers. The Internet is an integral part of Q Model Management. They use their web site, www.qmodels.com, to facilitate finding new models as well as booking clients.

Industry veterans Gwen Saiman and Jeffrey Kolsrud started Q Model Management. They and a team of experts manage male and female talent ranging from new faces to top models. It is very encouraging to know that such an innovative, progressive agency considers good old-fashioned common sense as important to high technology as it meets the needs and challenges of the new millennium.

Paul West has worked in the modeling industry or several years. Books he has promoted include *Male Superstars: The Men of Boss Models, Marcus Schenkenberg: New Rules* and *The Brewer Twins: Double Take*. Paul works with both agencies and individual models as a multimedia consultant for television and the Internet. He has a great deal of insight and advice for upcoming models. Discussing the pros and cons of the Internet, Paul had this to say, "Modeling is the new Hollywood. Little boys and girls grow up watching Entertainment television, MTV and CNN where the amount of fashion coverage is comparable to the amount of coverage given to other areas of the entertainment business. These young people no longer grow up wanting to be on Broadway or in a chorus line. They want to walk down the runways in New York, Paris or Milan. The Internet provides a phenomenal opportunity for them to send their pictures to agencies. There is, however, a phenomenal downside. Unscrupulous agencies are making a fortune from people's hopes and dreams. They are making money on so many young people who should honestly be told that they are too short, or not suitable to be a model."

I asked Paul for his views on the future of the male modeling industry. He told me: "It can only get more lucrative. I firmly believe that men are the women of the next century as far as culture is concerned. For the bulk of this century it has always been men in the positions of power and men have objectified women as beautiful. Now we find women in positions of power as producers, designers and directors. The male form is being objectified as beautiful. The tables have turned. The women's market is not necessarily going to grow substantially. For instance, there is not going to be a huge number of launches in women's cosmetics. The men's cosmetic market is wide open as is the men's fashion market for apparel. As we go into the next century, and men continue to become more savvy about what they are wearing and how they groom themselves, we will see an explosion in the market place. It used to be that wives shopped for their husbands. Now, husbands shop for themselves."

Paul had these words of warning and advice about the drug scene so prevalent among young models in New York: "The drug scene exists in any business. I'm from Houston and it exists in the oil business. It really comes down to the individual and how they are going to handle it. My advice to models is to remember that modeling is a business, not a lifestyle. Make a very clear distinction between work and play. No one is going to hire you because you have done drugs with them or gone out for drinks with them. The type of work you could get, you would not want."

Paul's advice to parents is: "If a model is still a teenager, the parents should be involved. They should know whom their child's agent and booker is. Many promising young models start when they are 18 years old, an age when they are sent off to university. A parent would not send their child off to a college they didn't know about. They should not send them to a model agency they don't know."

To obtain the current addresses of all of these and other New York agencies, I advise you to contact Peter Glenn Publications at 888-332-6700 to obtain the New York City Model Agency Directory. *This is an invaluable guide which pinpoints about 50 of the legitimate agencies. It covers, among other things, agency interview times and the types of models represented. Peter Glenn Publications also has a web site (www.peterglennpublications.com) which will have updates to the directory.*

Chicago

Chicago was not what I had expected. Hollywood had distorted my vision! I thought machine-gun-toting gangsters would lurk on every corner. (Well, I did see a gangster tour advertised!) As in every big city, there is a crime problem and wandering the streets at night is not advisable.

But Chicago is basically a happy, friendly city with beautiful Lake

*Michigan shimmering in the center. For models, Chicago is a good balance—
a big city with big city opportunities and a small town with small-town friendliness. It is the second largest market in the country and offers a wide range of
modeling. Here you will find print, high fashion, runway, showroom, television, catalog and fitting work.*

There is work for the perfect size model, as well as large sizes, petites
(not much I'm sorry to say), juniors and children, plus hand and foot models.
There is also a strong male market. And there is a constant flow of models to
and from Europe and Japan.

The fashion industry in Chicago has seen many changes in recent
years as a result of the financial failure of many catalog houses. Catalogs for-
merly provided most of the work in Chicago, but now the emphasis has shifted
to other areas. However, Chicago is still a good city in which to begin a modeling career. Agents are willing to work with new faces to develop them for
their own agencies as well as other markets. Yet, as in every other market, the
competition is strong and professionalism and patience are essential.

Shane Allen, a booker and director of scouting for a leading agency
told me: "The Chicago market has diversified tremendously in the past five
years. And the next five years in Chicago will be fascinating. It is and always
has been a catalog market but at the same time it is a great advertising market.
Editorial work is also picking up. Clients will pay between $1,500 to $2,500 a
day for high caliber models. For $3,500 they want a Star. When models come
through town with good books they get the lion's share of the work. There is
an Asian market and a huge demand for Hispanic models. Chicago is a very
diverse town."

Another agent told me: "The economy is rebounding, therefore people
are purchasing, therefore advertisers are advertising. The market is better and
stronger than ever."

After many successful years with her own agency, Susanne Johnson
merged SUSANNE JOHNSON TALENT with A-PLUS TALENT, a talent
agency which also represents large size models, to meet the needs of a diversify-
ing industry. "That was the way to survive," she told me. Susanne has strong
international high fashion ties. Her models work the Haute Couture shows in
Paris, Milan and London.

Katherine Tenerowicz handles Plus size models. "In Chicago that is
size 12 through 16. Height requirements are 5'8"(minimum) to 6'." The age
range has always been late twenties to early thirties. However, Katherine is now

getting more requests for younger models—girls in their teens and early twenties. "Sometimes I have trouble finding girls in that age bracket because teenage girls who are a Plus size still don't feel confident about their size. They feel insecure as opposed to someone who is a little older and more secure with their looks and size." She added: "The girls who are Plus size are in excellent condition. They work out and are well toned. They are concerned about what they eat. I treat their careers as I do the agency's regular size fashion model."

In Chicago, FORDtook over the well-known David & Lee agency in the spring of 1999. Noreen Threlkeld is director there. Ford is a full-service agency, with divisions in fashion, commercial print, acting, as well as others.

Long-time agent and scout Marie Anderson Boyd, who discovered Cindy Crawford, is co-owner of ARIA MODELS with her partner Mary Boncher. Marie firmly believes in being diversified—to a point. She said: "This agency is for men and women and has every division but runway and animals!"

ELITE, Chicago, is a high-fashion agency representing men and women. Elite sister agency for talent is STEWART TALENT.

The name Arlene Wilson is very highly respected in Chicago. Arlene retired in 1997 but her agency ARLENE WILSON MANAGEMENT continues under the direction of Michael Stothard. It is a full-service agency for men, women, children and plus-sizes.

There are other reputable, successful agencies in this city.

Dallas

Dallas is renowned for its beautiful women. The modeling industry here has grown rapidly in the last five years. It is mostly a catalog, commercial and year-round market and there is a great deal of runway and live trunk show work. All categories of modeling are represented. There are opportunities for the new model. It is also a good market for males.

The first model agency in Dallas was opened in 1961 by Kim Dawson. One of the first international models, Kim started her career with the John Robert Powers agency in New York. She was one of the first American girls to model the Collections for the famous couture houses in Paris. Kim told me: "There were no agencies in Paris at that time. We just made calls on the couture houses. They considered it a great status symbol to have an American model wear their clothes." When she returned to the United States and Dallas, she opened her own agency, the KIM DAWSON AGENCY. The business is a family affair. Kim's daughter Lisa, who also modeled in Paris, is the director.

Concerned about the large number of girls who enter the modeling profession (and particularly concerned about the models who go to Europe), Kim told me: "The modeling profession has had so much publicity in recent years that we have an overwhelming load of models in every market in the world—and there are not that many markets. The media hype has resulted in mothers who feel that their daughters just have to be part of this business. So often when a girl goes to Europe, it is the mother's dream that has come true and not necessarily the child's."

Kim is very direct when talking to models and their mothers about the business in Europe. She told me: "I stress that Europe is the beginning of a nightmare for many children—a lot of these young women are more child than adult. I tell them they are going to a culture that has a lot of drugs and sex. I am very honest with them because I have had too many girls come back to tell me horror stories of their experiences. If young people are well informed and well prepared and if they realize that their whole life is more important than the next five years, they will approach the business with a totally different attitude." On her life in the industry, Kim says: "It is a business to which I am enormously grateful. I have made a career in Dallas and my agency has made a difference in Dallas."

Lisa draws on her experience as an international model to pass on this advice to newcomers. "New girls have to be adaptable. When they go to Europe if they are told to cut their hair, or to use less makeup, they must follow instructions. Many girls from provincial markets will cry and get upset when they are asked to change their look. We can test them here and put together a portfolio. But if they can work and get tear sheets in Europe, they will do so much better when they come back.

This agency represents all categories of modeling.

Page Parkes brought an international flair to the modeling industry in Dallas and Houston. She went to school in London and attended the American School of Fine Arts in Paris. In Europe she scouted models for the Dallas market.

In 1979 Page and her business partner, Rachel Duran, opened the Page Parkes Center of Modeling in Houston, a testing and training facility for new models. This was followed by the InterMedia Model and Talent Agency, which establishes models in the local Houston market. The two women then took their expertise to Dallas, where they started PAGE PARKES MODEL'S REP, an agency designed exclusively for models with international experience. Page told me: "In Dallas we look for girls with special features. They must be at least 5'9", have beauty and have had editorial experience on an international level. Our goal is to make them stars." Model's Rep, which now has a sister agency in Miami, provides personal service and representation for a select group of high-income models. It also ensures a high standard of professionalism for clients.

The name Mike Beaty is well known and respected in international circles. A former model and an agent, Mike contributes kindness and integrity to the business. His MB MODEL AND TALENT EXPO, which takes place in Dallas and other locations annually, offers great opportunities for new models (see Chapter 18).

THE CAMPBELL AGENCY, CLIPSE MODEL MANAGE-MENT and the DALLAS MODEL GROUP are also among good agencies in the city.

Phoenix

Phoenix is primarily a catalog market and is definitely seasonal— October through May being the best time for work. Domestic and foreign clients and international photographers work there because of the beautiful climate and locations. It is a good market for fledgling models who live in the area but others are not encouraged to move there. Good tear sheets and work experience in Europe are essential. There is also a market for the large size model.

Robert Black who owns the FORD ROBERT BLACK agency said: "This is a growing market. My agency has expanded to meet the needs. We have divisions for runway, commercial print, fashion print and children. Our talent department handles radio, television, film and hair and makeup artists. Height requirements for women are 5'8" to 5'11" and for men, 6' to 6'2". These statistics apply to the whole area."

There are several hard working, successful agencies in Phoenix and Scottsdale.

Los Angeles

Los Angeles is one of the world's most competitive markets for agents and models. Many new agencies have failed in recent years as a result of major financial problems in the fashion industry. There is a super abundance of models and the majority have all of the necessary qualifications. The big allure is the movie industry and the opportunities for television. Top models who can demand and receive big booking fees in New York often prefer to make Los Angeles their base in the hope that they will make the overnight, lucrative leap from model to movie star or celebrity. In the meantime an established model can get direct bookings for assignments in Milan, Paris, Germany, London, Japan and Australia.

The look for models in this city is very varied. While grunge is out and classic is definitely in, the range is wide. As one agent said: "The look here is not only classic, but different and exotic with some models sporting tattoos and shaved heads. Our models range from geeky, weirdo, to classic, editorial." There is strong competition for male models. Los Angeles abounds with male actors who have had successful modeling careers in New York, Paris and Milan. Agent Ken Steckla told me: "Male models have to be prepared to travel a lot, in this country and overseas. We have many foreign clients—at least those not scared away by fire, riots, earthquakes and mudslides! We look for men who can do newspaper, catalog and television work as well as a wide range of products, with emphasis on swimwear and athletics."

I discussed the industry with Kurt Clements, an agent who has been in the business for many years. He said: "In Los Angles the industry has such a wide range. There are so many looks that sell."

Los Angeles is a good place for a model to begin but on a small scale. Clients are conservative and won't take the chance of using a new model for a big campaign. Gerard Bisignano has experience as an international model and agent. He told me: "In Europe or New York people will take the gamble with a new face because they want to be able to say 'I discovered this person.' Here it is very rare that a model will take off and make money quickly. Clients want models with good portfolios. A model can start in L.A., but then he or she has to go to Europe or New York for experience. When they are more competitive they can come back here to work."

Gerard is concerned about the moral welfare of young people who choose modeling as a career. "In any industry where there is youth, beauty and a lot of money to be made, there is certainly great room for abuse. It is important that parents give their children a long-term spiritual foundation, with strong moral principles and a good sense of self-worth. With this type of background young people will realize that compromising their value is not the way to achieve success. If an agent suggests a moral compromise, a model will know that he or she is at the wrong agency."

Nina Blanchard was the First Lady of the industry on the West Coast. Her retirement came in March 1996, after 34 years in the industry. Nina's original ambition was to be an actress and she went to New York to achieve this goal. "When I knew I could not be a Joanne Woodward, I gave up the idea. I'm glad I realized this when I did, otherwise I would still be a waitress in New York hoping to become an actress." Nina has this advice for young models and actors: "For years I have heard people say they are insecure. Everyone is insecure—if you are not insecure, you are dead! Don't drain your emotional energy on negative thinking or anger. Spend it on things that matter. Use your emotional energy to do something with yourself."

Nina wrote a book about the modeling business ("It's fiction of course, or I'd get sued!") She is now a personal manager. Her advice and opinions will always be highly respected.

In March 1996, the world famous Nina Blanchard Agency was sold to FORD MODELS in New York. FORD L.A., as it is known in the business, represents men, women, children and large sizes. The main emphasis, however, is on managing the careers of its models-turned-movie stars and on launching the acting careers of its high fashion models. There is also an accent on the sports model.

Heinz Holba is a powerful name in the industry here and abroad. An agent for years, Heinz opened L.A. MODELS in 1985. His new ideas, technique and credibility attracted clients from all over the world, creating a year round market for Los Angeles.

Jason Otto has always been "fond of fashion and the modeling business" and decided to open his own agency, OTTO MODEL MANAGEMENT, in 1992. Talking about the industry changes in Los Angeles he said: "More fashion photographers are coming to L.A. and we are seeing more location shooting. This means more work and greater competition for the models." Jason looks for men "who are healthy, athletic, muscular but slim." Height requirement is 5'11" to 6'3". Age range is 20 to 35. Height for women is 5'8" to 6'0". Age range is 15-20. The agency also represents hair and make-up artists. There is a strong commercial division as well as fashion and print.

ELITE/L.A. opened in 1979 as the West Coast headquarters for the giant Elite Model Management Corporation in New York. With a worldwide network of model agencies at its disposal, this agency can find the appropriate markets for all its models. It has a men's division and represents models for film, print, catalog and television work.

Among other highly reputable agencies, are: C' LA VIE MODEL AND TALENT AGENCY, WILHELMINA MODELS, NEXT, AGENCY

2000 and MAJOR MODEL MANAGEMENT.

San Francisco

When the weather is cold in Europe and New York, clients find San Francisco a perfect location because of its climate and beautiful scenery.

Lynn Claxon, owner of the very successful STARS, THE AGENCY, had this to say about the market: "San Francisco is an ideal place for a model to get her feet wet and to get used to living away from home for the first time. It is smaller and more personal than New York and we have excellent photographers here. Although this is mainly an advertising town, there is a broad spectrum of work that includes fashion, theater and television." Lynn's husband Colin, an entertainment lawyer, (see chapters six and eight) and their children Kristin and Scott own the agency. Kristin is director of fashion and Scott is in charge of new faces and scouting, here and abroad.

As parents, the Claxons relate to the concern of other parents whose daughters are starting careers away from home. Lynn says: "We make every effort to brief them on what they must expect in this business. We are particularly concerned about girls who have never been to Europe before. We tell them what they should and shouldn't do and what to be aware of. As their mother agent we make sure that we deal with only the most reputable agents and we keep abreast of what is happening within the business around the world. Stars is based on hard work and a very high standard of integrity."

The height requirement for girls is 5'8" minimum and the age requirement is twelve to twenty-one. Very young girls stay at the Claxon home. Men must be 6'0" or over.

Among other good agencies are CITY MODEL MANAGEMENT and MITCHELL MODEL MANAGEMENT.

Seattle

Seattle is a significant scouting ground for agents from all over the world. I asked many of them why the Pacific Northwest attracted such attention. The consensus of opinion was that the beautiful climate and Scandinavian influence produced tall, healthy, strikingly beautiful girls who have "the clearest skin in the world."

This is a very friendly community and there is great rapport between clients and models. There is a lot of fashion show work here as well as catalogue, advertising and television. Models can also work in Los Angeles and San Francisco, which means they can work three markets at one time. A model's career span is longer in Seattle. When models have worked internationally they can return and work for a considerably longer period than in other cities.

There are several reputable agencies and modeling schools in the area. This city is an ideal place to learn about the modeling profession and launch a career. It has excellent liaisons with other American agencies and with top foreign agents.

Atlanta

Atlanta is a sophisticated, beautiful city especially in the Spring when it is awash with dogwood. It is mainly a catalog market but there is some editorial, advertising and television work.

There are many good agencies. One of them is L'AGENCE, whose president is tall, good-looking Mark Cook. Mark and his mother Gretta, who is also his partner, run a highly organized international business. Mark told me: "Atlanta is an easy transition for girls from the southeastern United States who plan to eventually work in New York or Europe. It is a great place for new girls especially in the summer when most of them are out of school. There are good testing photographers here and a good client base." Describing the type of model represented by his agency, he told me: "The look for women is fresh, tall and beautiful. Height requirement is 5'9" to 5'11". New models must be under twenty-one years of age unless they have been well established in another market. The look for men is clean-cut, athletic and they must have very good bodies. They should be eighteen and over. Height requirement is 6'0" to 6'2" and the size for men is 40 Regular to 40 Long." This high fashion agency has commercial print and television divisions. It also represents Plus size models (size 12 to 16 with the same height restrictions as for regular size) and handles actors and actresses.

Shay Griffin is a former model, an agent and has a good perspective of the industry. She said: "Atlanta is an international city and consequently our business is becoming more and more international."

Take time to check out other reputable agents in Atlanta. A full range of modeling is available through them.

Miami

A beautiful coastline, sun drenched backdrops, superb models, agencies that provide a full range of facilities and worldwide publicity from television and film have contributed to Miami's rise from regional to international status. Clients from France, Italy and Germany shoot catalog and print work in the area for six months of the year, making this region the largest market for fashion photography in the country. The prime location, South Beach, once a very run-down area, is now home to the chic, avant-garde and jet set.

The Florida fashion production season runs from September until May with the peak months being January, February and March. These famous photographers Steven Meisel, Patrick Demachelier and Bruce Weber arrive to shoot with the world's supermodels. International photographer Mac Hartshorn discussed some of the reasons why photographers like Miami so much. "First of all, it is a beautiful place to shoot. During the winter the weather is perfect most of the time. The days are longer because it is close to the Equator. The air is very clean. The light is different. It's hard to know why but it has something to do with the atmosphere. It is crisp. The sunset and sunrise photographs are incredibly beautiful."

The effects of a devastating hurricane, crime against tourists and declining foreign currencies were thought to have taken a toll on Miami's fashion market. The market, however, is as stable as ever, producing thousands of catalog shoots per season.

The MICHELE POMMIER and IRENE MARIE agencies were the first to contribute to Miami's modeling success. Tremendous promotional efforts were made to German and other international fashion clients. For catalog photographers, there is no better place to shoot than in Miami. All the support services needed can be found within a two-mile radius in an area known as South Beach. These include the first class modeling agencies such as ELITE, FORD, NEXT, KARIN and PAGE PARKES, as well as high-end film labs, production vehicles, hotels and, most importantly, a large pool of modeling talent. A good model with a good book and a lot of tear sheets can expect to earn $1500 a day. Experience is important. Many of these photographers spend a lot of money per production. Time is of the essence and there is not a lot of room for error. There are more models than jobs in the Miami market and agencies are becoming more strict about who they sign on.

I asked Michele Pommier what advice she would give to the hundreds of aspiring young models in Miami. She said: "Modeling is a serious business.

It is not a world playground. You can make good money if you are a true professional. Keep good hours. Leave partying for the weekends. Listen to someone you trust in the business—preferably your agent. Remember what your mom and dad taught you. If someone approaches you with drugs or improper suggestions—just say no!"

Tampa, Orlando and Brevard County

These are local markets and they illustrate how young boys or girls who dream of becoming models can achieve this goal provided they have potential and a good local agent.

In winter, clients from Canada and Europe come for the warm climate and beautiful settings this area offers. Universal Studios opened in Orlando in 1988 and MGM followed. Other film companies produce here. The Disney Corporation provides a constant source of print and television commercial work for local talent. Lucy Heim, who owns MDM Studios, a modeling school in Brevard County, is a board member of the Space Coast Film Commission. She told me: "the film industry is booming in Florida. By the year 2000 our goal is to bring in a billion dollars to the State."

One of the prime figures behind the international spotlight in Florida is Dott Burns, who opened her agency in Tampa in 1970. Dott is a remarkable woman who has a great sense of humor and an indomitable spirit. She was the mainspring behind the legislation that requires all agents in Florida to be licensed by the state. Explaining why she spent four years trying to get this bill passed, she said: "There were one hundred unqualified people acting as agents in Florida. There were no rules and there was no discipline. Bona fide agents and talent suffered as a result. This bill got rid of the scams and rip-offs."

Dott was a successful model and fashion illustrator in New York before coming to Tampa to be married. She had a daughter, Kim (an actress) and later began a career in television. This ended abruptly when a serious illness brought her close to death and confined her to a wheelchair. "One never knows what is going to happen in life. For this reason a model should always be prepared to do something else—to have an alternative means of making a living." Her agency is very successful, but Dott claims that she would not be in the business today it if were not for the friendship and support of top agent Eileen Ford. "Some years ago, I was feeling discouraged and didn't think I could continue in the business. Eileen wrote me a scorching letter telling me to get my act together, that she expected more of me than to think of quitting. I felt that if a woman of her standing thought I could make it, then I would. And I did. Eileen is a great lady."

Susan Scher, a former international model who owns the very successful ALEXA MODEL AND TALENT AGENCY in Tampa, scouts for the famous KARIN agency in Paris and New York. There is also the JAZZ AGENCY and the BOOM MODEL & TALENT AGENCY.

Agencies in Orlando include THE BODY SHOP, BAILEY'S MODEL MANAGEMENT, INC. and UNIQUE CASTING.

Aspiring models on the east coast of central Florida are fortunate to have the expertise of Traci Danielli, president of the BREVARD TALENT GROUP. Traci has a thorough knowledge of the New York modeling industry and has connections with agents all over the world. She is part of a very successful mother-daughter team. Her mother, Lucy Heim, opened MDM Studios, Inc., in 1981. This is a licensed school in which the curriculum encompasses music, drama and all areas of modeling. MDM is an excellent example of how a modeling school should be run; not only for its legitimacy but also for the opportunities it provides its students.

Chapter 8

International Modeling

Canada

Canadian models are in demand all over the world. Canadian agents are held in high esteem by their international colleagues. Professionalism, friendliness and a certain élan keep Canada in the forefront of the world of fashion. As I traveled through the fashion capitals, I was so impressed by the praise for this country and its models that I decided to explore the industry here.

Toronto is the major market and Montreal is next. Other cities such as Ottawa and Vancouver are growing markets, especially Vancouver which has an impressive film industry.

One Paris agent told me: "I do most of my scouting in Canada. Every time I go there, I find star material. The models are fantastic and the models and agents are friendly and so professional."

The average earnings for a model are between $60,000 and $80,000 (Canadian). A new model can earn $30,000 (Canadian) and a top model $150,000 (Canadian). A foreign model with haute couture experience and correct working papers (obtained by the Canadian agency) can earn $60,000 (Canadian) in three months.

Toronto

There is editorial, catalog, runway, print and commercial work in Toronto.

Height requirements and other criteria match those of other fashion capitals. I asked agency owner Alecia Bell why Canadian models receive such rave reviews all over the world and she said: "Canada is a melting pot of ethnic backgrounds. We have communities of Ukrainians, Poles and Scandinavians. Height, beautiful bone structure, wonderful hair and skin are in the genes." Alecia gave me her views on why the modeling industry has progressed so rapidly in the last few years: "We have several high-quality fashion magazines in Ontario. Our photographers are widely recognized in the international market. The trend is for photographers to apprentice in Europe. They bring their skills back to Canada and become very competitive. In Toronto testing is comparable to, if not better than, Paris. Models can get fabulous tear sheets here. International agents go wild about our pictures."

GIOVIANNI MODEL MANAGEMENT, FORD CANADA, ELITE and ICE MODEL/TALENT MANAGEMENT (this also has a very successful school) are among a number of first rate agencies in Toronto. PLUS FIGURE MODELS/LITTLE WOMEN MODELLING AGENCY is Canada's only agency specializing in plus and petite sizes. Jackqueline Hope, Canada's first plus size model, owns it.

Montreal

European influence, a lucrative market, good photographers, major fashion magazines and a good client base provide excellent opportunities for work and tear sheets.

Corrine Poracchia, an agent and former model and stylist, told me: "There is a lot of catalog work here. We have excellent photographers, which makes this a good place for a model to start a career. But this is a comparatively small market. A model with good potential must be prepared to travel. Foreign agents scout in Montreal and the opportunities for an international career are good."

GIOVANNI MODEL MANAGEMENT is known and respected worldwide. Another successful agency is FOLIO.

Vancouver

Canada's third largest market offers catalog, print, runway, film and television opportunities. The market is very competitive. Agents groom models for Europe, Asia and the United States.

Charles Stuart Quest, a former model who started his agency CHARLES STUART INTERNATIONAL MODELS AND TALENT in 1982, has models working in all of these markets. Lissa Lloyd and Thomas Gusway (Tom also co-owns Mitchell Models International in Los Angeles with Jobee Yoshizawa) are major players on the international fashion circuit. Their special focus is on the Asian market. They have tremendous knowledge of that particular aspect of the business. Other agencies include LIZBELL MODEL MANAGEMENT and BLAST MODEL AND TALENT MANAGEMENT.

••••

International modeling can be a glamorous, exciting, fulfilling experience. It can also be a painful, lonely, devastating end to a dream. Hundreds of unqualified, unsupervised, hopelessly naïve girls flock to Paris and Milan every year hoping to break into a modeling career. These are the girls who have major problems.

Before you attempt an international modeling career, you must have: a) the basic qualifications, b) a knowledgeable mother agent who knows the international market and deals with reputable agents, c) maturity and emotional stability to cope with the demands of the profession and, d) a thorough awareness of what you are getting into. Read this book thoroughly. I have traveled all over the world and interviewed the most experienced people in the business. If you know what to expect and are prepared, you will have overcome a major obstacle.

The agents who will establish your international career are the agents who are in the fashion capitals—New York, Chicago, Los Angeles, Dallas, Phoenix, Atlanta, Miami, Munich, Hamburg, Zurich, London, Paris, Milan, Madrid, Tokyo and Sydney. These agents work together. Many agents in small towns and satellite markets do not know or understand the profession on this level. You must deal closely with an established agent in one of these major cities. Do not, under any circumstances, attempt to go to Europe under your own steam. It is imperative that you work through an agent in your native country. Write to the big agencies. Send them photographs and request an interview.

Why does a new model have to go to Europe? Europe is the finishing school of modeling and agents have slightly more time to mold a career. There is also a greater concentration of magazines and fashion houses than anywhere else in the world. This means greater opportunities to get tear sheets.

Here is some important advice. When you go to Europe do not expect to work right away. For the first six months do not measure success in terms of tear sheets and money—these will come in time. Remember that the experience of living and surviving in a foreign country is in itself a measure of success, and also a powerful form of education. This is an outstanding opportunity to become a world traveler, learn languages and study other cultures while learning the basic essentials of your profession. You will learn patience, how to cope with rejection, how to budget your finances and how to smile and congratulate a friend who got a job instead of you (when inside you are crushed with disappointment and resentment). Until you learn all of this, you will never be a good model or have any hope of surviving in the profession.

Here is one encouraging fact: after many interviews worldwide, the one thing that impressed me was that the people at the top really care. The masterminds who own and run the world's top modeling agencies do care about their models, especially the newcomers. Some top people were models themselves. Some are parents. They too have experienced homesickness, success, rejection, fear and doubt; but keep in mind that these people lead hectic lives and they certainly do not have time to babysit. A new generation of model agents is arriving on the scene. They are people who have spent years learning the business with big agencies in New York, Paris, or Milan and have now started out on their own. They have witnessed models' scarred egos and have learned from other agents' experiences and mistakes. Their agencies are small, allowing them time to be good at what they do while still showing compassion for the newcomer. Some models do best with a small agency; others are less easily intimidated by the size of a large agency.

It is very important that you check credentials of any agent with whom you deal. There is no room for naivete in this profession. Don't be afraid to ask questions about your career. Your quest for knowledge will be respected.

The following information will keep you up to date on economic developments in Europe and how it affects models and agencies to some degree. The 1992 unification of Common Market countries saw a free-trade agreement among members of the European Economic Community (EEC). It enables Europeans to work in any member country they choose with little formality for working papers or permits. American models, however, still must adhere to immigration laws. There are advantages and disadvantages to this change in Europe. But one thing is certain—the language barrier will remain unchanged!

Legal Aspects of International Modeling

Colin Claxon, attorney and co-owner with his wife Lynn H. Claxon of Stars, the Agency, in San Francisco (see the chapter on legal matters), has this to say about the legal aspects of international modeling:

"Your agent in the U.S., the "mother" agent, usually arranges to place you with an agency overseas—Paris, Milan, Tokyo, for example—and will receive a referral fee or percentage of the commission paid to the foreign agency. A good mother agency closely monitors your progress overseas, as often as weekly. You should report all problems with your foreign agent to your mother agent. Never switch foreign agencies without first consulting your mother agency. All agencies differ and some may not be right for you, your look, or your career. If you feel that a change is required, discuss it with your mother agency and let them make the arrangements. European agencies compete voraciously for models and it is not uncommon for "runners" to hang around the front of agencies handing out cards and promising to make young models "Stars". Avoid them!

There are strict laws regarding work in a foreign country, which may prohibit or severely restrict what you can do. Before you leave the U.S., ask your mother agent to explain any foreign work restrictions to you. Your agency should obtain the required clearances, or explain what you have to do to work overseas.

Living expenses and a small allowance are usually advanced by European agencies and some provide housing. It is not unusual for them to mark up their expenses above the actual cost. Some will collect full apartment rent from each model who shares an apartment, reaping a large profit. Don't stand for this. Find out the actual cost; complain and report it to your mother agency.

Always request an accounting of your expenses at least every month and keep your own records of your bookings and earnings each day. Make the foreign agency verify your earnings. Never wait until you are leaving to attend to this. It always seems at such a time there is no one available to answer your questions.

Many European agencies will advance round-trip airfare to Europe. An advance is a loan and will be deducted from your earnings.

If you make insufficient money to cover your expenses, the European agency will not expect you to reimburse them, if you have maintained your weight, have devoted sufficient time (usually two to three months), have worked hard and followed their instructions. You are a risk that they take, an investment and if they fail to produce sufficient bookings to recover their costs, it is their loss. On the other hand, if you are discharged for misbehavior, if you change agencies, quit, or return home because of home-sickness and the like, some agencies may attempt to recover their expenses by billing you, threatening legal action, or putting pressure on the mother agency. Reputable agencies have a zero drug tolerance policy and will discharge you immediately if you are involved in any drug related incident. Violation of local laws, some of which may be vastly different from what we know in this country, can result in not only termination, but also deportation. Stay in touch with your mother agency and report and discuss any such incidents with them immediately.

Most foreign agents properly deduct foreign income taxes, social security and health taxes. Always get an explanation of these deductions. In countries like Japan, these deductions and the agency commission can total 50% of the gross earnings, but you will still make substantial money. Keep a copy of everything relating to your jobs: vouchers, tear sheets and releases, etc. You may one day have to prove that you didn't authorize use of a photo."

Now we will travel to the fashion capitals, explore the markets and talk to the top agents in the business. A final word of encouragement: American models are held in high esteem around the world for their professionalism, friendliness and team spirit. Keep up the good work!

London

British fashion has, as one editor put it "always straddled the divide between edgy street fashion and lofty tradition." Whatever the eccentricities, London has become an impressive force in the fashion world. Designer collections have more than doubled in size and importance on the international scene.

London is unique. Steeped in history and tradition, it is elegant, sophisticated, exciting, cosmopolitan, slightly eccentric and enormous fun. It is a tough city for a model. Agents are selective and precise in what they want and expect. London has superb photographers and big business accounts. To keep pace with the high level of activity and degree of professionalism, agents prefer girls with experience. In Paris and Milan agents will make allowance for inexperience if a model has potential and will take the time to train her. This is not the case in London, where time means money. An inexperienced model will not work or make money quickly.

London agents are straightforward, honest and efficient. They arrange work permits for foreigners and explain commissions and other financial details very clearly. I interviewed several agents in order to get a good overall and fair picture of the London scene. The people to whom I spoke have been in the business for many years. While they differed on specific requirements, they all agreed on the need for a model to have money, insurance, grooming, personality and to be well behaved. Their comments gave an excellent picture of the modeling scene.

One agent who has been in the business for close to thirty years was concerned with the number of American girls who arrive in Europe "on the flip of a coin." She told me: "Agents in America tend to tell girls that if they go to Europe, they will work instantly. School directors should take a tour and find out what is going on in Europe and Japan. American models should bring with them at least $2,000, medical insurance and a return ticket. They must behave professionally at all times and have a lot of self-discipline."

The rules concerning modeling in the United Kingdom are laid down in a red book entitled Terms, Conditions and Standards for the Engagement of Professional Models in Still Photography. This is published jointly by the Association of Fashion, Advertising and Editorial Photographers, the Association of Model Agents and the Institute of Practitioners in Advertising.

Height requirements in London are 5'9" (with a few exceptions—we all know about supermodel Kate Moss who is 5'7") to 6'0" for women; 5'11" to 6'2" for men.

Carole White and Chris Owen, a brother-and-sister team, ran their own agency, Premier, in swanky New Bond Street before merging with the famous Elite organization to form ELITE PREMIER. At the time Chris told me: "Our vast knowledge of the local market and its top international models are a totally winning combination. Our high profile and the large volume of work make us the strongest agency in London."

I asked Chris how the economic unification of Europe had affected models. He said: "English and American models can move freely throughout the European Economic Community (EEC) and there has been a major breakthrough for American models. We can obtain a full working visa for them within four weeks. This is automatically renewable after a year. This can only be done through the main modeling agencies in London.

London is an excellent market for male models. The look for men is young and modern and models travel constantly to Paris, Milan, Germany and Japan. Carole told me: "For a man, modeling is not a fleeting career. It can last a long time. Men don't take it quite as seriously as women do. They use it as a tool to see the world. I think this is the right attitude. If a man does it for vain reasons, it puts people off. Clients don't like vain men."

I asked her for advice for new as well as experienced female models. She said: "They must be ambitious. A model must work with us on a fifty-fifty level. It takes as much effort on her part as ours. A girl should see modeling as an important career that will allow her to travel all over the world and make an incredible amount of money. She must become professional very quickly, make money and invest it well. She must think ahead. In five years it will be over."

Carole told me that foreign girls obtain work quickly in London. "Clients know that a new face will only be in town for a short while and they want to see her." Her advice to potential models is: "Be confident! Take dancing and acting lessons. Learn how to move well. Know your look. I suggest that you save a few outfits you will feel great in to wear to go-sees. Take special care with your makeup. Even if you have a good book, you must be well turned out all the time. Clients are human. They want the girl in front of them to look as terrific as the girl in the book."

Chris is very active in the Association of Model Agents, which negotiates fees with clients on behalf of model agents. He said: "When we are negotiating, we have to keep in mind that a girl has about five years to make money and invest it. Once it is over, she is not likely to have the opportunity to make the same kind of money again. She doesn't know anything else, because she hasn't had the time to learn any other business. When agents receive complaints from clients that a model has been late for an appointment, we take disciplinary measures. But we have to remember that a model is not a tube of toothpaste or a can of beans. She is a human being who can make mistakes. We have to take all of this into consideration when we are negotiating fees." Chris now divides his life between London and New York where he runs Mission, the special projects division of Elite. He handles special events, endorsements and campaigns for such supermodels as Linda Evangelista, Claudia Schiffer and Naomi Campbell.

Top agent Clare Castagnetti feels that American models traveling to Europe for the first time should go to London first in order to avoid a language barrier. "If girls are not secure, the culture shock will be overwhelming. Paris and Milan will really throw them if they are not prepared. It makes life so much simpler if they can understand the language. This business is tough enough as it is and it is getting harder. Unless a girl is totally dedicated, she is wasting everyone's time. This is a very serious business."

Another very successful agent, Gabriella Palmano takes hundreds of telephone calls from would-be models every month, interviews only about eighty of these girls and accepts only one! I talked at length with Gabriella. Here are her comments on a number of aspects of the business. "There is a lot of hype on the street about how bitchy models are and how photographers want to get every girl into bed. But that is all it is—hype! "A lot of girls don't realize what a strenuous and demanding career modeling is. Being photographed all day is hard work physically.

"It is important for a girl to know that personality is fifty percent of the business. It is as important as looks. If a girl is beautiful and a pain in the neck to work with, she will be booked once and never again. A girl who is not as beautiful, but who is bright and has a pleasant personality, will be booked over and over again.

"A model always has to look her best—even if she has had a fight with her boyfriend and has been up all night crying. She can't come in to the agency the next day looking and feeling a mess. A girl with a desk job might get away with it, but not a model. She must always be in top form."

April Ducksbury, a well-known and respected model agent, also had very definite opinions and advice. She told me: "We are very selective when we accept girls from overseas. We generally know who will work, but we can sometimes make a mistake. If a girl from the States doesn't work after three weeks, we call the mother agency, explain that her look isn't right for us and arrange to send her to a market that will suit her better. If she is not up to our standards, or we think she is totally hopeless for Europe, we tell them this also. We are very truthful with the agencies.

"American agents should check all details very closely when they send girls to Europe. A number of agents do this, but many don't. It is very dangerous for a girl to just arrive in a foreign country. She wanders from agent to agent— even country to country—is not accepted and then has to go back to America. I think this is terrible. If the proper arrangements have not been made, they haven't a chance of working. It is a waste of their time and it breaks their hearts. I feel so sad for them."

April explained that payment from clients in London for an assignment is usually delayed for three months. Consequently her agency will advance sixty percent of the invoice amount the first day a model works. Fifteen percent is kept in reserve in case there is a problem with clients concerning unprofessional behavior on behalf of the model, or to pay leftover bills from a model's doctor or dentist. The other twenty-five percent consists of the agency's twenty- percent commission and a five- percent fee for advancing money. April told me: "A model does better financially in London than in Paris or Milan. In Milan, the agencies take fifty percent and the girls find it difficult to find out just what they are earning, even if they are given a piece of paper with a lot of figures on it."

She strongly emphasized the importance of a model having a good personality. "Models must be professional, polite, well behaved and easy to get along with. Sometimes models behave very badly. We hate it when they start getting spoiled and stupid. If a model gets a reputation for being hard to work with we will ask her to leave. If there is the slightest inkling of drug use, they are out immediately. We don't want girls who are a bad influence on other models. Our reputation is at stake too. There are a lot of people involved and we are all in this together. American girls have incredible determination and their attitude toward becoming a model is the same as if they wanted to be a doctor or an accountant. However, we have found that when we have put them into a home to live with a family, they are very unhouse-trained, very undomesticated. An English girl is much quieter, much more considerate." On the subject of male modeling she said: "It is a very serious career for a male. If he is well groomed, charming, has a great personality and gets on well with clients, he can work for a long time."

Sarah Doukas opened her immensely successful agency STORM in July 1987 after a prestigious career as a booker. Although she has many success stories her most famous is probably the discovery of Kate Moss in a standby line at Kennedy Airport in 1988. Kate was fourteen at the time and 5'5". She is now 5'7" and despite her height is one of the greatest models in the world—thanks in great part to Sarah! Sarah told me: "Our models have a specific look. We accept girls who will fit the Elle and Vogue market. But personality is very important. Even if a girl has all the physical attributes I might not take her if she doesn't have a good personality." Storm's men's division was opened because male models in London wanted to work for Sarah as soon as they heard she had opened an agency. She accepted only a few at the beginning, but as work increased the division was permanently established. "We have two categories— the classic man and the very interesting editorial man. Again, personality is a top priority," said Sarah.

MODELS ONE, SELECT and NEXT are among the reputable, successful agencies in London.

General City Information

Transportation: **Airports**: There are two major airports serving London—Heathrow and Gatwick. When you arrive at either one you will clear Customs by a) following a red sign if you have goods to declare, or b) following a green sign if you do not. Warning: do not make the wrong decision! Customs officials make regular spot checks in the green division. Heathrow: The Underground (also called the Tube) connects this airport with all Tube stations in London, including the main British Rail stations. Service is excellent and the journey to the city center takes forty-five minutes. Cost is very reasonable. The Airbus, a double-decker red bus, goes into the city every ten minutes and takes about fifty minutes, rush hour traffic permitting. There is plenty of room for luggage. There is also a green coach (bus) service called Flightline 767. **Taxis**: London is famous for its taxis. Fares are posted inside. The fare from Heathrow to the center of the city is roughly twenty pounds, depending on traffic. Drivers have a mind-boggling knowledge of the city. This is helpful for a model who is new in town, but taxis should not become habit-forming; they are expensive and the Tube is often faster, especially in rush hour. There is an extra charge for each piece of luggage or additional passengers. **Tube**: This is the name given to the subway. You can buy one-way or round-trip tickets and daily, weekly and monthly passes. Anything exceeding a daily pass requires a card bearing your photograph. This can be purchased at Victoria Station and is a must for models. **Buses**: The best way to see London on your days off or when you have time is by the famous double-decker buses. Ticket conductors ride on the buses and tickets are interchangeable with Tube tickets. They can also be bought separately. There are a number of tours which can be boarded at Piccadilly Circus, or at Hyde Park corner. The best of these tours is the one that advertises "Original Tour of London." It takes about one hour forty-five minutes. The English are very orderly about lining up for buses. A bus will automatically stop at a compulsory red sign. If, however, a bus stop sign has REQUEST written on it, put out your hand to stop the bus. **Cars**: Beware! Cars drive on the left side of the road. Look to the right before crossing.

Currency: The pound (£) sterling is the monetary unit. It is made up of 100 pence, referred to as "p." Money comes in bank notes and coins. Check these closely until you are used to the currency.

Banks: You get the best rate of exchange at a bank. Every major bank has branches all over London. Hours are 9:30 a.m.-3:30 p.m. Mon.-Fri.; off-hour service is available at the airports.

Telephone: Models live on the telephone! City code for London is 171, but drop this when dialing within the city. Always put 1 in front of any city code. To call an international operator, dial 155. For local calls, the newer phones are easy to use. If you have a number of calls to make, you can deposit a coin and the amount you have used will appear on a small screen. However, if you do have to use one of the old telephones, a little explanation will be useful. (I still find them nerve-racking!) Dial the number first and then as soon as the party at the other end answers (an English person will either say "Hello" or is more likely to say his own telephone number) you will hear a series of fast pips. You will think you have been cut off, but you have not. Quickly deposit the required coins (the amount will be posted) and be sure to give them quite a push to make them go through the slot. The connection has now been made. Another series of horrid pips will sound when more money has to be inserted. I warn you this system is ghastly! To make a direct call to the United States, dial 010+1+area code+number. Parents or friends calling London from the U.S. dial 011+44+171+number for a direct call. The international code is 011; 44 is the country code; 171 is the city code for central London, 181 for outer London. A collect call is called a "reverse charge" call and can only be made from a private phone. If you don't have a private phone, you can go to the Westminster International Telephone Bureau, 1 Broadway, SW1, to make a direct call and pay at the end of it. Hours are 9:00 a.m.-5.30 p.m. including weekends. This can also be done at Trafalgar Square post office and at both airports at special telephone offices. In an emergency situation, dial 999.

Postal Service: Main post office: 24-28 William 1V Street, WC2N 4DL. Tel. 239 2000. Open twenty-four hours seven days. Regular post office hours are Mon.-Fri. 9:00 a.m.-5:30 p.m. (sometimes 6:00 p.m.)

American Express: Central office is located at 6 Haymarket, London SW1. Tel. 0171 930 4411.

Tourist Information: Visitorcall is the London Tourist Board's 24-hour service. Tel. 08391 123456.

Embassies/Consulates: **Canada**: Canada High Commission, McDonald House, 1 Grosvenor (pronounced "Grovenor") Square, London W1X OAB. Tel. 0171 258-6600. **U.S.A.**: 24 Grosvenor Square, W1A 1AE. Tel. 0171 499-9000.

Toilet: Do not refer to a toilet as a bathroom. People will look at you in amazement. I heard one snooty hotel doorman ask an American gentlemen who inquired as to the whereabouts of the bathroom: "Does sir wish to take a bath?" This facility is called a lavatory or toilet. Signs outside read W.C., LADIES, or GENTLEMEN.

Time Difference: London is on Greenwich Mean Time, except during May through October when clocks are moved ahead one hour to establish British Summer Time. GMT is five hours ahead of Eastern Standard Time in the United States.

Water: Water can be drunk from the tap (faucet) all over England except for some trains, where signs will indicate otherwise.

Electric Current: 220 to 240 volts, AC. You will need a converter unless you have dual voltage equipment and an adaptor for British sockets (outlets). These can be bought at major department stores or electrical shops.

Recommended Street Map: Agencies recommend the "A-Z," which includes a Tube map.

Language: English. *For the benefit of American models, here is a list of words that have different meanings:*

American	British
pantyhose	tights
raincoat	mac
dieting	slimming
apartment	flat
umbrella	brolly
flat (as in tire)	puncture
shot (medical)	injection
drugstore	chemist or pharmacy
elevator	lift
sidewalk	pavement (American friends thought I was weird when I told my children to play on the pavement.)
trunk (of a car)	boot
hood (of a car)	bonnet
cookies	biscuits (models must never eat them!)
candy	sweets (nor these!)
check (restaurant)	bill
gasoline	petrol
truck	lorry

Note: In Britain, when the date is written, the day comes first and then the month, e.g., 2/1/99 is January 2, 1999. In the United States it would be written 1/2/99.

Police Emergency: Telephone 999. No money is required. The same applies when you dial "0" for operator assistance.

Shopping: Stores are open Mon.-Sat 9:30 am-5: 30 PM or 6:00pm. They do not close at all during the day. Wednesday and Thursday nights some stores close later in certain areas. Some stores open on Sunday afternoons.

Tax: V.A.T. stands for Value Added Tax which is applied to all purchases. When you strike it rich and get lots of work you might find yourself on a shopping spree. If you spend over a specific amount in certain stores you can claim this tax at a later date, by filling out forms. It is worth the trouble, so be sure to keep receipts.

Sightseeing: This is not meant to be a guidebook by any means. However, as this city was my home for many years, I have to urge you to do and see certain things. You will never be bored in London. Many sights can be seen at little or no charge. There are a number of tours leaving from Piccadilly Circus. The best tour advertises "Original Tour of London," and takes about two hours. See the Changing of the Guard at Buckingham Palace and Windsor Castle. Go to the Royal Mews to see the ceremonial coaches and carriages. Don't miss the Tower of London and take a ride down the Thames. Jump onto the open-air double-decker bus in Piccadilly and do an inexpensive tour. Spend a day in Harrods, the world's most famous department store, "just looking"; another day at Hampton Court. Museums are a must; afternoon tea, a tradition. Go to the theatre—tickets can be bought at half-price the same day as the performance, in Leicester (pronounced Lester) Square. I could go on and on. Oops! Almost forgot—don't go anywhere without your brolly (umbrella) or mac (raincoat)!

Germany

Germany is the biggest fashion exporter in the world. Hamburg and Munich are major markets and have a high concentration of catalog work. Some of the work is done in studios, mostly because the weather is undependable. A large part is also done in the United States. Miami and Phoenix provide all the necessities—including beautiful weather.

Once established, a model can earn reasonable money, pay expenses and live well. However, this is not really the country for tear sheets. Most of these will be unsuitable for portfolios in Milan or Paris. This can be frustrating, but the situation is improving. You should also know that television commercials are extremely limited. Therefore you cannot rely on this medium to supplement your income to any extent. There is a big market in Germany for male models.

Germany runs on rules. It runs efficiently, to the benefit of everyone. So do the agencies. Obey the rules and you will be successful. Break them, or try to bend them and you could be sent home.

A German girl is expected to finish high school and university, or an apprenticeship to a trade. Parents insist on this. As a result, there are few German models. By the time they have finished their education it is too late to start. It is unheard of for a girl to take a year off from her studies to model and then return to school. And as a general rule German men don't model. Hence, the demand for foreigners.

VELMA, an organization of licensed model agents in Germany was started to protect young models from disreputable businesses calling themselves model agencies. Before answering MODELS WANTED type advertisements, potential models can call the VELMA headquarters in Munich to find out if these people are members of the organization. VELMA scrutinizes credentials of agencies applying for membership.

The two major cities in which models work are Hamburg and Munich. There are excellent agencies in both cities. Let us take a look at each city.

Hamburg

This is an ideal place for young models to start in the profession on an international level. Parents can relax and breathe a sigh of relief if their son or daughter signs with an agency here. It is very safe, low key, conservative and sophisticated. The people are friendly and most of them speak English. There are no muggings and few robberies—a portfolio left in a restaurant will be there two days later. People in the profession are honest. A deal is a deal. The look here is young, fresh, girl-next door. There is not only catalogue work in Hamburg; there are several magazines that provide constant work for hair, body and beauty products.

I interviewed Sebastian Sed, an Englishman, who was a model agent in Germany for many years. Sebastian invented the Sed Card—the composite that is a model's indispensable work tool. He voiced the same concerns of agents all over Europe today about problems confronting new, young models. He told me: "They have the very wrong idea that once they have arrived here everything is going to be easy. They expect too much. They think this is a sure road to success and they are going to be stars. This is probably the fault of the people who run the modeling schools."

I asked several agents how long it takes for a girl to start working. The general answer is that the commercial model who is tall, has a good smile, beautiful hair and the right look can work after ten days. She will always be right for catalog. The editorial girl who is more extraordinary, more exotic but not necessarily beautiful, tends to be more successful—eventually. She can take six to nine months to get started. That is the hard part. Agents admitted that some girls don't make it at all.

Eileen Green has all the charm and humor of the Irish and a beautiful brogue to match. She has a wealth of knowledge of the history of the business and the people who founded and developed it. Eileen was an agent in Hamburg for many years. She had this to say: "Before they leave home, girls should be told, by their modeling school director or their agent, to respect the country they go to and to learn something about it. Europe is a great learning experience."

Concerned about girls who arrive in Hamburg overweight and who try to solve the problem by crash dieting, she said: "This is a great danger. It is better for a girl to stay at home and lose the weight sensibly. It is very frustrating for a model to lose a job because she is too heavy. She must be honest about her measurements. Clothes are made to a certain size and it is terribly sad when a client wants to book a girl who has a super look and then finds out that she is one or two sizes larger than the size she has printed on her card. It is awful if this results in her being sent home at her own expense."

On the subject of rejection, Eileen said: "There are so many reasons why a model might not be booked. She must never take it personally and become depressed." On the model/agent relationship her advice is: "A modeling agent offers a service to a model for a fee. The combination of model and agent must be good. Both must be happy. I advise any young model to shop around and if she is not happy, to change agents. The agent also has the privilege of asking her to leave."

Eileen advises young girls who have never had to live on a budget to ask questions about rent, transportation and food and to forget about buying clothes until they are working and covering expenses. She emphasizes that models from overseas must have travel and health insurance and, as a further security measure, enough money to support themselves for at least a couple of months. Money should always be in the form of travelers checks. "Modeling is a gamble. These young people are not walking into security," she said.

Mention the MODEL TEAM agency to anyone in the business and it is acknowledged with admiration and respect. It was opened by Sonja ("Soni") and Ralf Ekvall, a Swedish couple, in the seventies and is the oldest model agency in Hamburg. It is large, with 400 models on the books; half of the 250 girls are American. The strong male division is also very successful. Soni is tall, striking and elegant, with a keen eye for talent. Her judgement is seldom wrong. She looks for girls who are 5'9" to 6'0" tall, with long legs, excellent hair and skin, a good smile and who are "skinny enough." At her agency a little variation is allowed on the perfect 34-24-34-body statistic. Girls who have slight measurement problems are told to swim and work out in a gym. Men are warned about playing too many sports or doing too much bodybuilding; muscle-bound legs and very broad shoulders are a no-no. Soni explained: "There is a great deal of fashion here, a great deal of catalog work, but models have to be able to fit into the clothes."

Asked about her keen sense of judgment in selecting models, she said: "When I see a girl I can tell instinctively if she is good. The way she presents herself to me is the way she will eventually present herself to her client. Of course, even when I am convinced, I can be wrong. A girl might be very homesick and very unhappy and if this is the case, she will not present a positive image to the client. If a girl does not do well and I have to send her home, she does not have to repay her fare. I consider that my investment—a business investment. It is very, very unusual that a girl doesn't work at all because I am so picky when I make my original selection."

When a new girl arrives at Model Team, a lot of time is spent teaching her the agency's policy, how the business works and about Hamburg itself. Soni told me: "I was a foreigner here once. I know it can be frightening for a young girl. A good agent will tell her models that she believes in them and makes them feel happy and confident. A lot of success lies in planning. When I know a foreign girl is coming, I ring up good photographers, good hairdressers and get clothes for tests. I treat it as if the girl were on the job." She added: "If a girl arrives with a good book she can work within a few days. If it has to be changed, it will take her two weeks. There are a lot of good magazines here. It is a very big market." Specifically, Soni stresses the need for a model to obtain health insurance prior to leaving home.

Pia Kohles is an agent, booker and scout and runs the BODY and SOUL agency. Explaining the advantage of wearing these various hats, she said: "At every agency the bookers know what type of model clients want because they have direct contact with them. Scouts don't work with the clients. They travel, find cute girls who don't necessarily work and the whole thing becomes a disaster. In my case, I scout girls around the world knowing what clients are looking for and when I get back to the booking table I know who is coming to the agency. I have met the girl. She arrives within two months and she works. I have never had a problem. Very occasionally I have brought a girl to Hamburg having only seen her book. Then I have found that she looks different in person. We are disappointed. Things don't go well. The girl is disappointed and the mother agent is too. Again it is a disaster."

Discussing the problems of teenagers arriving in Europe in pursuit of a modeling career, Pia told me: "Every year hundreds of young girls come from America and Canada and go to Milan during their summer break. They sit there with three pictures in their books and it is a waste of time. Eighty percent of these girls don't have a chance in Milan. It would be much better if they came to a smaller agency in Hamburg where there is a lot of constant work in catalog, beauty, body and hair. Agents will advise them to go to Portugal, or Greece to work on their books and then come back to Hamburg for more experience. Then they can go to Milan and Paris.

"When new girls arrive at Body and Soul, they have an in-depth discussion with a staff member during which they learn about the agency and the city. They are accommodated with a Hamburg family. Everything possible is done to launch a successful career."

Body and Soul only represents women.

The following information is typical of the type of information given to models by agencies all over the world. It gives insight into how an agency operates and what is expected.

Hamburg Hints

1.	Full-day Booking	Nine hours including lunch.
2.	Half-day Booking	Four hours, approximately
3.	Overtime	The first half-hour is "give & take" and thereafter each hour is chargeable. Agency must be informed within 24 hours of the booking for overtime to be negotiated. Please make a note of agency booker.
4.	Expenses	Trips outside of Germany, clients usually pay most expenses including hotel/lunch, etc. Flight bookings within Germany, client pays hotel and breakfast only, plus any taxi expenses incurred in the city or town of work.

Taxi expenses in Hamburg to the airport are not chargeable. Expenses are paid only if all hotel and taxi bills are received by the agency within 5 days of booking completion.

5. Traveling Time — Catalogs do not pay traveling time if the booking is for five days or more. Editorial or advertising trips are negotiable re traveling time.

6. Cancellation — For single-day booking models must cancel minimum 48 hours before day of booking. For more than single-day bookings, models must cancel equivalent to the length of the booking (i.e. with a five-day booking the model must cancel at least five days before.)

7. Accessories — Girls are expected to arrive at all bookings fully made up, with clean hair and with bodystockings, etc. Any other accessories will be given as an extra with booking details.

8. Go-sees — Go-sees are generally arranged in mornings in the agency, never over the phone.

9. Cash from Agency — Generally Thursday & Friday only, between noon and 3 p.m.; for special arrangements phone agency

10. Cash from Client — If cash is paid by client for fee/flight, etc., a full breakdown of the total amount must be given to the agency within 24 hours.

11. Next-day Bookings — Agency must be phoned before 5:30 p.m. (17:30)

12. Trips Abroad — Models are responsible for visas (phone your consulate), passport and vaccinations. Beware: Any model not showing for a booking is liable for

the day's full production cost, including other models' fees. Not showing for a trip also includes liability for all flight, travel and hotel costs plus fees incurred by client, photographer, stylist, other models' etc. The model will be sued in country of residence or the costs deducted from model's account. Any model late for booking loses not only the hourly rate for the late time, but also must pay other models' waiting time.

General City Information

Transportation: Airport: Hamburg's airport, Fuhlsbuttel, is seven miles from the city and is linked to the city center by taxi or a combination of bus and subway. You will find the bus stop to the left of the exit doors on the lower level of the airport. The Airport Express bus leaves every ten minutes for the Ohlsdorf station, which is serviced by the U-Bahn and S-Bahn trains. A train for the desired destination can be taken from there. **Taxis.** Fare begins at 3.60 deutsche marks (DM). Fare is DM 2.20 per km plus 50 pfennigs for each piece of luggage. If you call a taxi by phone, the meter will start a little higher. It is not considered correct behavior to hail a taxi from the side of the road. One must find a taxi stand, or call 040/441-011, 040/686-868 or 040/611-061. **U-Bahn.** This is the name given to the underground or subway system. Tickets for the rapid-transit trains, serving the Underground and S-Bahn local lines can be purchased on a single or daily basis at any station. A weekly or monthly pass, which requires a photo card, can be bought at the Hauptbahnhof, which is the central station. The last two are not recommended by agents for models who plan only a short stay in Hamburg or who travel constantly, back and forth, to other countries. I am going to outline the procedure for buying a single U-Bahn ticket, because on my first day in Hamburg, I traveled all over the city without one. I just did not know how or where to buy it and I could not find an official to ask. Here is a step-by-step description: At the station there is a board with a list of numbers next to a board with a list of destinations. Find your planned destination and press the corresponding button. The cost of the journey will be shown and you can insert the correct amount. Paper money is not accepted. A daily ticket is represented by a button with a T on it. Press the button; the ticket price will appear and you can insert the correct amount. **Buses**. Tickets may be purchased from the driver and they are interchangeable with daily U-Bahn tickets. **Cars**. Vehicles drive on the right side of the road.

Currency: The deutsche mark (DM) is the unit of currency. One deutsche mark equals 100 pfennigs, or DMl = 100 pfg.

Banks: Mon., Tues., Wed. and Fri. 9:00 a.m.-1:00 p.m. and 2:30 p.m.-4:00 p.m. Thurs. 9:00 a.m-1:00 p.m. and 2:30 p.m.-6:00 p.m. Closed on weekends.

Telephone: Making a telephone call can be a challenge in foreign cities. In Hamburg, I met a couple of models who, every morning, in order to check in with their agency, had to get up, dress, walk (usually in the rain) several blocks to the nearest telephone box and, clutching the correct change, stand in line to check in for the day! There are locks on many apartment phones and models may only receive incoming calls. Long Distance: It is possible to dial direct; e.g. for the United States dial 00+1+area code+number. A collect call can be made only from a private phone or at the main post office. Dial 0010 and you will hear a voice say: "Bitte warten Sie," which means, "Please wait." When you hear the next voice, ask for an international operator. Long distance calls can be made from the Hauptbahnhof. Specially marked phone booths will enable you to make international calls, but you will need to have a great deal of change. You can also buy a phone card. Phones that have their numbers clearly printed on the outside can be used to receive calls. Parents or friends wishing to call Hamburg would dial 011+49+40+number. The international access code is 011; country code for German is 49; city code for Hamburg is 40.

Postal Service: The post office in the Hauptbahnhof central station is open twenty-four hours. Other post office hours are: 8:00 a.m.-3:30 p.m.

American Express Office: This office is located at Ballindamm 39, Tel. 040 309-080.

Embassies/Consulates: U.S.A. : Alsterufer 28. Tel. 040 411-710

Toilet: HERREN (Men), DAMEN (women)

Time Difference: Hamburg is one hour ahead of Greenwich Mean Time (GMT), six hours ahead of Eastern Standard Time (EST) and nine hours ahead of Pacific Standard Time. Daylight Saving Time is in effect between April and September.

Tipping: Service is included. If service is outstanding, a small additional gratuity is appropriate. Porters: DM3 per bag. This is a good tip for any service.

Water: Water is safe to drink except on trains.

Electric Current: 220 volts, A.C.

Recommended Street Map: The Falk Plan

Police Emergency: Telephone 110

Munich

Munich is the capital of Bavaria, the beer capital of the world and the fashion capital of Germany. The German name is Munchen, which means Place of the Monks. The Munchners are hard, dedicated workers who make a point of taking time out to enjoy life. Oktoberfest, the beer-drinking festival and Fasching, a carnival that lasts from the Epiphany on January 6 to Mardi Gras or Shrove Tuesday, are world-famous festivities that draw crowds from all over the world. Models, designers, photographers, makeup artists and stylists crowd into Munich during Mode Woche—Fashion Week—which takes place in March and October.

Life is pleasant, easygoing and safe and considerably less formal than in Hamburg. Models love this city, but they have to be really good at their profession in order to work here. The situation in the business has changed in the last few years. At one time, for example, it was considered chic to book an American model because it was a different thing to do. This is not the case anymore unless the model is very good. Clients are not eager to work with beginners. They will pay high booking fees, but they insist on value for money and that means experience. It is definitely not easy to get tear sheets here. And the idea that a new model can make money quickly is totally wrong. One booker took time out from a busy schedule to have coffee with me and give me some insight into the business. She emphasized the disillusionment young models face when they arrive in Munich as a result of misleading information given to them before leaving home. "It is very wrong of agents in other countries to tell girls that if they come to Germany they will make enough money to go to Paris and Milan to get tear sheets. This idea is very wrong. The fact is, you need tear sheets to do catalog work here."

The height requirements in Munich are a minimum of 5'8" for a girl—although as every agent will tell you anywhere in the world, there is always the exception to this rule. Sometimes a girl who is 5'7" and in some way absolutely outstanding will work constantly. But I do emphasize that this is not usual. A male model must be 6'1" or a little taller. In Germany and Switzerland, models are expected to bring their own makeup to jobs and know how to apply it well. They are also expected to have their own accessories.

A model does not need a fabulous book but it must be good and show that she has experience. She must be easy to work with. Clients will not tolerate arrogance or lack of professionalism. In fact they will happily pass over a beautiful girl for one less pretty with a great personality. Time is money. They want to get the job done quickly and well and enjoy doing it at the same time.

I spoke with Louisa von Minckwitz, a journalist and former model who opened her agency, LOUISA MODELS in Munich in 1981 and in Hamburg in 1990. We discussed changes in the business in the last few years. She told me: "The business has become harder and more competitive for everyone. There are more agents, more scouts and many more models. But Germany is still very safe. It is not like Paris or Milan. We don't have playboys with invitations to parties." Louisa firmly believes that a girl should finish high school before embarking on a modeling career. "She needs an education so that she can go to university, or do something else. You never know what is going to happen with a modeling career."

I had the pleasure of interviewing at length agent Ingrid Reiling who was very concerned about the misconception with which new girls arrive in Munich. "Girls are told by agents that they can come here to do catalog work without having a book. This is just not so. It is very difficult. A couple of years ago clients would call us and ask us to send over a few girls. Now they ask to see a card first and then, if they are interested, they will ask to see the girl and her book. If the book isn't good enough they won't book her."

Modeling is extremely competitive in Munich. Clients are always looking for new faces and they can choose from models who flock into the city from all over Europe and America. There really are many beautiful German girls and their sense of fashion is innate. But amazingly enough, they look down on modeling as a profession. It doesn't have the same prestige for them. Ingrid explained: "The term model has a different connotation here. If a girl says she is a model anywhere else in the world, everyone thinks it's fantastic. It is every girl's dream. But here I have to convince a girl to become a model. I have to bring her to the agency and prove to her that we are professional and that she can be serious about her work."

We talked about how the business has changed. "At one time a girl had to be beautiful. Now all kinds of looks are in—even ugly! It is very strange for an agent to see a girl who she thinks is ugly but whom she feels has a chance.

Heide Themlitz, a soft-spoken, extremely charming agent has been the power behind the TALENTS agency. She voiced her concerns about new models arriving in Europe. She explained that Americans have the toughest time for a number of reasons. Europeans are used to traveling from country to country and dealing with different cultures and languages. Americans are not. European models know that in Germany they must have their own accessories and make-up, which they must know how to apply expertly. Americans generally are not aware of this when they arrive.

These points are very important in this country. Another major point that Europeans seem to be more aware of is the need to have money in order to survive until they work. Heide told me: "American agents should prepare girls for Europe. They send them to Milan, where they can't possibly work without good books. They don't have money, become depressed and gain weight. They sit around and nobody cares for them. American girls are pushed into the profession at a very early age. They don't know how to handle it and many of them don't know how to behave properly. We always have problems when we rent them an apartment. We have problems with their telephone bills. And they don't have much respect for other people's possessions. They do not receive good advice from their agents in America. Models must never arrive in Europe without money. That is why they become involved in the drug scene."

Summing up, then, we can say that Germany is an excellent place to break into the international modeling scene provided you have enough money for accommodations, food and tests for a few months. If you do not have a reasonable book or reasonable pictures, you must be prepared to be very patient until you get them. Be pleasant, courteous and respect the people and their culture. If you do this you will have a terrific experience, learn the business from experts and be on your way to success.

General City Information

Some of the details for Munich such as currency, water, electric current etc., will be the same as for Hamburg. Please refer to that section. Below are the points that differ.

Transportation: Airport. The Franz Josef Strauss (FJS) Airport is $17^1/_2$ miles from the city center. The S-8 S-Bahn links it with the city's main train station.

Telephone. The city code for Munich is 89. To make international calls, follow the same format as for Hamburg.

Postal Service. Main post office is at the Hauptbahnhof central station and is open twenty-four hours. Always make sure that you have the correct postage for airmail.

American Express Location is Promenadepl. 6. Tel. 089 290-900.

Embassies/Consulates: U.S.A. Koniginstrasse 5-7. Tel. 089 28880

Zurich

Zurich is the fashion capital of Switzerland. It is also the country's largest city and banking center. It has tremendous Old World charm and is truly delightful. Life is conservative and the Zurichers are organized and to the point. Sometimes their efficient, businesslike manner is mistaken for arrogance and coldness. This is not the case. They are extremely courteous and helpful. You, in turn, must be polite, punctual and professional.

This is probably the best city in Europe for an experienced model to make excellent money. A beginner, however, will not do well. There are few photographers for testing and a model must have a strong book and tear sheets to prove that she is experienced. There is very little editorial work. Television advertising is minimal and poorly paid. This is the city for catalog and commercial work.

Here is an important point: models must have their own accessories and makeup and know how to apply it well. This is imperative for catalog work.

Official papers are essential for living and working in Switzerland. Everyone pays taxes. Agency fees range from 25 to 30 percent and include commission, accident and health insurance and the 8 percent government tax.

Zurich has a serious drug problem. Imprisonment and/or deportation are the penalties. Agencies will not tolerate the slightest sign of drug use.

There are no underground trains and taxis are expensive. It is wise to learn the bus and tram systems quickly. The service is excellent, easy and inexpensive.

Switzerland is bordered by France, Italy and Germany. The look that is "in" for these countries is "in" for Zurich about two months later. Foreign models are in demand. Swiss men do not model, which makes Zurich a great city for male models. American men are popular. However, the Swiss do not consider modeling a "proper" profession for a girl. She is expected to finish school and university, by which time it is too late to start a modeling career.

Françoise Rubartelli was first a model and then an agent for many years in Zurich. She laughed when she recalled her decision to become a model despite protests to her parents from relatives and friends. "My parents were asked: 'Your daughter is from a good family. Does she really need to do this?'" Her career decision was definitely frowned upon.

During our interview, Françoise expressed her concern that models are getting younger and younger. She told me: "In Milan, I have seen fourteen- and fifteen-year-olds sitting on staircases drinking milk. They were not working, couldn't speak the language and were so lonely and unhappy. I blame the parents for this terrible situation."

We discussed the problems facing models trying to start out in the business in Zurich. Françoise explained: "It is very difficult for a beginner. She has to start somewhere, but it can't be Zurich. A good book and tear sheets are essential. At one time we were flooded with fifteen- and sixteen-year-olds who had good portfolios because they worked with a good photographer in America. But they came here without accessories or makeup and hadn't a clue about how to handle themselves. The clients were angry. A model is not usually booked from her book, but if she is, she had better be good. When Swiss people get mad, they get mad and they don't forget!"

Longtime agent Judy Stauble had this to say about the business in Zurich. "This is a pure money market. It is catalog and advertising work, not editorial work. Here models start in their teens—by their mid-twenties their careers are more or less over. A man's career lasts longer. My advice to young people starting in the business is to be very careful and to listen to different people before they make a career decision."

Marianne Fischer is another very successful agent. When we met she was exceedingly gracious and eager to offer advice and information to help a model feel at home in Zurich and work as much as possible. She also emphasized the need for a strong book and tear sheets and sends models to Milan for tear sheets if necessary. Marianne explained: "Switzerland is the best place, moneywise, for a girl who is experienced. Zurich is small and models soon get to know each other, so there is no problem with homesickness. There is a lot of work here and time passes quickly."

If a girl is experienced, she can arrive in Zurich with about $300. If she has not worked within a month, she is advised to relocate.

Height requirements for modeling in this city are 5'9" to 5'11" for women and 6'0" for men.

General City Information

Transportation: **Airport**: Zurich Airport is about seven miles from the center of the city. There are taxi, bus and train services. **Taxis**: These are expensive and models are advised not to use them. **Underground**: There is no underground system. **Buses and Trams**: This system is cheap, efficient and easy to learn. To buy a ticket, find a vending machine and find your destination, which will be in the red, yellow, or blue areas displayed on the machine. Press the appropriate button and the fare will light up in red. Insert the correct number of coins. Single or daily tickets can be bought at each stop. Weekly and monthly tickets are not advisable for models who are planning a short stay. They take the form of a photo card, which is obtained at the Central Train Station. Anyone found traveling without a ticket will be fined on the spot. **Cars**: Traffic drives on the right side of the road.

Currency: The unit of currency is the Swiss franc (SF or F). One Swiss franc equals 100 rappen. Money can be changed at banks, travel offices, the airport and Central Station (6:20 a.m.-11:30 p.m. daily).

Banks: Hours are 8:15 a.m.-4:30 p.m.

Telephone: The country code is 41. Dial 191 for international numbers and information. For direct calls to the United States, dial: 00+1+area code+number of party. Parents and friends wishing to call Zurich from the U.S. dial: 011+41+1+number. You cannot dial overseas from a pay phone. This must be done at a post office. Make the call and pay at the counter.

Postal Service: The main post office is Sihlpost. Hours are: Mon.-Fri. 7:30 a.m.-6:30 p.m. Sat. 7:30 a.m.-11:00 a.m. Sun. closed. All other post offices close for lunch. There are special weekend and emergency hours at the Sihlpost and at the Central Station post office.

American Express: Office is located at Bahnnhofstrasse 20. Tel. O1 211- 83- 70

Embassies/Consulates: The embassies are in the capital city of Bern. Canada: Kirchenfeldstr. 88. Tel. 031 352-63-21. U.S.A.: Jubilaumsstr. 93. Tel. 031 357-70-11.

Toilet: DAMEN (Ladies); HERREN (men) or MANNER; TOILETTEN; or W.C.

Time Difference: Zurich is one hour ahead of Greenwich Mean Time (GMT) and six hours ahead of Eastern Standard Time (EST). It has Daylight Saving Time also.

Tipping: Restaurants include 15 percent plus tax on the bill. A tip of 1SF or 2SF is still expected after a small meal.

Electric Current: 220 volts, AC.

Recommended Street Map: Offizieller Stadtplan Zurich und Umgebung. This map includes the bus and tram routes.

Police Emergency: Dial 117.

Language: The official language in Zurich is German. English is widely spoken. As France, Italy and Germany border Switzerland, French and Italian are also spoken.

Paris

Paris is chic, exciting and romantic. Love and fashion are its greatest exports. The Parisians have a passion for life and enjoy their leisure time with as much Gallic gusto as they do their work. The older generation is deliciously arrogant on the surface, but gracious, charming and extremely receptive once introductions have been made. The young do not have this aloof veneer and are easily approachable. And, as is always the case with the young, they make friends easily with their contemporaries.

Paris fashion has had a dynamic impact on the world, thanks to the creative genius of Dior, St. Laurent, Chanel, Courrèges and many others. Frenchwomen are brilliant at accessorizing, but they would look chic in a sheet and Wellington boots! A young model can learn a lot by looking at the store windows on the Champs-Elysées or sitting in a sidewalk café watching the parade of fashion go by.

An organization known as Le Syndicat des Agences De Mannequin (S.A.M.) gives the guidelines to agencies for rates, rules and regulations and defines the laws on royalties, television and poster rates.

Certain documents are required in order to live and work in France. It is mandatory that you have these and that they are kept up to date. You will hear the words "social security," or "securité sociale" frequently when you arrive. I was confused by the meaning of this until I discovered that French social security is not the same as American social security. In France, it is the term given to reimbursement by the government for medical expenses. (However, a model must have completed eight work assignments in a month to be reimbursed. This is the law.) Each agency delegates a staff member to handle working papers for new models. This task is handled diligently. A breach of the rules will result in the prosecution of the agency and the deportation of the model. Think twice before you change agencies. When you do, the documents become invalid and you have to start all over again with your new agency! These facts strongly emphasize that one cannot drift from one European country to another hoping to obtain work. American models do not need a visa to enter France. Don't forget to take your birth certificate to Paris! This is essential for obtaining official papers.

Social security, mandatory tax and some insurance deductions, as well as the agency's commission will be deducted from your salary. The model/agent relationship is different in France. The model is the employee and the agent the employer. The agency is responsible by law for taking out taxes and having a valid contract. In the United States, a model works as an independent or freelance contractor. In France, another point of law is that sixteen is the minimum working age. The government keeps a close watch on agencies. One agent told me: "We have to prove that we are legitimate. France is scared about prostitution. Some 'agencies' have taken girls from Russia and the Far East for this purpose."

Models flock to Paris from all over the world for the Haute Couture (January and July) and Prêt-à-Porter (March, September and October) months. August, however, is vacation time for the French and all model agencies close.

Paris is a city for all models, from the beginner to the highest paid. The large, well-established agencies teem with activity and bookers sit with telephones at each ear, switching from one language to another with incredible ease. It is an amazing sight and their knowledge of languages never ceases to impress and humble me. The big agencies can be overwhelming for some newcomers who might be intimidated by the hustle and bustle. For these people there are good smaller agencies This is something you should talk to your mother agent or school director about before you leave home.

Height requirements for women in Paris are 5'9" to 6' with occasional exceptions. For the Collections, a girl must be at least 5'9" and the maximum hip measurement is 34". Height for men is 6' to 6'2". All categories of modeling are available for both sexes

In Paris a pleasant attitude and professionalism are as important as a good figure and face. Clients and photographers want to work quickly and efficiently. Time is money and tantrums are not tolerated.

Paris is an expensive city. New models should have sufficient money to support themselves for the first three months. For Americans, that is about $1,500 to $2,000. At this early stage you will not have tear sheets. A few good pictures will be sufficient. Once you are working, you will need three portfolios. The reason for this is that clients are tired of mile-long lines and insist on preselecting models from books before the final interview. Having three portfolios is not only an expensive proposition but also a difficult one. Foreign magazines are hard to find in Paris, so if you have worked in other countries, these foreign tear sheets may be hard to collect. Photographic prints are expensive. There are, however, good copying machine businesses in the city and your agency will tell you where to find them. There are over sixty model agencies in Paris. In the last few years the number of agencies that have closed for economic reasons is staggering. Locations, telephone numbers and staff members are on the move regularly.

Here is one very experienced agent's view on modeling in the city of lights: Paris is still the first market in the world and everyone wants to come here. There are so many girls here, each one prettier than the next. When I bring girls to Paris, I tell them the truth from the beginning. This is a cruel profession. Modeling is hard work for everyone. And I am very, very selective. They can't go to a party on the weekend and show up the next day with bags under their eyes for a photographic shoot. I warn parents and mother agents to know the agents they are sending the girls to in Paris. Problems happen so easily. A girl should go to New York first and work through an agency there.

"There is so much pressure on a new model. Her agency should be like a family, like a second home. Otherwise a model's life would be impossible and she would go home after a few weeks. I feel very responsible for the girls I work with. I advise them, groom them and mold them and I am very happy when they succeed."

I interviewed many agents in Paris. They all voiced deep concern about the welfare of fledgling models in their city. Renée Dujac Cassou is a beautiful and highly respected agent on the international scene. She believes that young girls should not go to agencies run by men. "Women owners are more professional. They are less competitive; they don't take girls away from each other." I asked Renée what factors determine a good agency. She said: "Good agencies have 'stars.' They are well organized and well financed. There are over sixty agencies in Paris. Only fifteen of them are good."

Véronique Marot, a former agent in Paris, is very aware of the culture shock experienced by young people who have never been to Europe before. "They must be ready to come—ready to cut the strings with home. Also, Paris is very expensive and they must be aware of that. If girls are really serious about modeling, my advice to them is to find an agency that is run by a woman. Many agencies are run by men who like to have their courts of young girls around them." Véronique stressed the high level of competition in Paris. "Certain things set a girl apart—good manners, a nice disposition, good features, beautiful hands, nice skin, good posture and great energy. That is what it takes. But even then she must be patient. There are girls who will go on appointments for three months and get nothing. They become so discouraged. Then suddenly it clicks. Some girls don't make it for a couple of years. I remember once, when I was with a big agency, I sent a girl who I thought had a definite potential to a photographer. But he called me and asked me why I had sent him such an 'ugly' girl. At that point I questioned my own judgement. Now, two years later that girl is on television and everyone wants to work with her. She is everywhere. In this business you just never know when it is going to happen. Sometimes a girl's career takes off right away. This is rare—and if it does happen like this it often fizzles."

I spoke with Jerôme Bonnouvrier who co-owns the DNA agency in New York. He owned agencies in Paris for many years and his information is very valuable. Asked about the problems facing young men and women starting careers in Paris, he said: "The main problems are generated by the new situation of being away from home and family in a totally new environment with a different language. The type and severity of the problems depend on the agency receiving the models. Models and their mother agents should carefully check the agency that will represent them in Paris. I think, however, that many models who are in trouble in Paris would be in trouble at home anyway. The best solution for young models is to feel the support of family and friends even from far away." I asked Jerome how long it would take for new models to a) work and b) make enough money to be self-supporting. He replied: "It could take from one day to never! On average it takes from five to ten weeks to work and three months to a year to make enough money to live on."

Nicolas Fiani, a television producer in Paris and an international scout who was a model agent there for twenty years, told me: "There are three important factors in the making of a model. She must first have the gift God has given her—the looks. Secondly, she must have a professional agency that believes in her. Thirdly, she must have the willpower. This is a serious business. It is also a tough, tough business. I see some girls make it and other girls with equal potential fall completely apart because they do not have the willpower to cope with the demands. They must always be beautifully groomed and always be on time. And they cannot party very much."

International scout Monique Corey said: "You can't be an amateur when you do this job. It is a vocation. In America girls can wing it a little bit. In a foreign country it is very difficult. I strongly advise young girls to take $2000 to Paris. Then they can take care of themselves until they make money."

Mahé Macaire is the scouting director for one of the leading agencies for men and women in Paris. Mahé endorsed Monique's views on financial independence. "A new model may not work for a long time. There are so many things to be anxious about, money should not be one of them."

Mahé knows her business well. She was a top international model for fifteen years. She was discovered by John Casablancas ("His parents lived close to mine in Geneva.") who signed her to his Elite agency. She told me: "I was afraid to go to Paris, so I went to Elite in New York." Tall, beautiful and unspoiled by her phenomenal success, Mahé had this advice: "Every girl dreams of becoming a model. They must understand the pressures involved and the rejection. If they don't, they will become depressed easily. Family support is a great help for their self-confidence." Mahé also feels strongly that if a model's career has not taken off after a year, their agent has the responsibility of telling them to think about a different line of work. "There is a lot more than modeling in life."

Nathalie Cros-Coitton has one of the newer agencies in Paris; she is an absolute delight—warm and friendly with an excellent background in the business. She worked for two of the most famous agencies in the world for a total of fifteen years before opening her own, the NATHALIE MODELING AGENCY. She has about 100 models, all women, 30 of whom are in town at one time. "I believe in strong management for my models. I respect them and as I am a mother myself I treat them as if they were my own children." Nathalie feels very strongly that her models look and feel healthy. "They must sleep well, eat well and take care of themselves." For her agency, she looks for girls who have "lots of natural elegance but are not too sophisticated. I look for girls who look innocent and have something magical about them. They must have good character, personality and charisma." Her advice to parents is: "Speak with your daughter's agent. Understand how the agency works. If a girl is not happy with or sure about her agent, she will be disappointed in her career." Her advice to models is: "If you have problems with people in the business who are not good people, tell your agency and parents immediately."

Nathalie agrees that if, after a certain time, it is obvious that a girl does not have the capacity to be a model, her agent has the responsibility to tell her. She also feels that a new model should have $1000 a month to support herself until her career is under way.

There are many excellent agencies in Paris. Among them are: KARIN, NEXT, CLICK, BANANAS MAMBO, CRYSTAL, ELITE, IMG, MARILYN, MADISON, THE PH ONE GROUP (which includes ABSOLU, an agency for women) and FORD FRANCE.

General City Information

Transportation: **Airports**: There are two major airports. Roissy-Charles-de-Gaulle is fifteen miles north of the city center. A bus leaves the airport every twenty minutes for the city terminal at Porte Maillot. The ride takes about forty minutes. There is also a train for the Gare du Nord station in the city every fifteen minutes. Orly airport is in the southwest of the city and about nine miles from the center. A bus leaves the terminal at Invalides every fifteen minutes. There is also a train to the Quai d'Orsay, Saint-Michel, or Austerlitz stations every fifteen minutes. A bus service connects the airports. The trip takes about one hour and fifteen minutes. There is also a helicopter service between airports and the city. **Taxis**: Taxis are available and expensive. They are always available and fares are registered on the meters. There is an additional charge for luggage. Other fare additions are posted. **Métro**: This is the name of the underground train system. You can buy single tickets or a book of ten, which is called a carnet. This may be also be used on buses. There is a bus, train and metro pass, which is an orange card bearing the owners name, signature and photograph. The weekly pass is called Carte Orange Hebdomadaire and is valid from the first to the end of the month. These cards provide very economical means of travel. **Now a word of advice**: Paris is a hectic city and the Métro can be overwhelming for the newcomer who does not speak French. Take the time to plan your journey to and from your destination. It will help you to know that the destination given for each of the many underground routes or lines depends upon the most distant destination to which that train travels. So if you see on a map where you wish to go, by following that train route destination you will then know what sign to look for on the Métro. Write the information in a book (you will probably use the same directions over and over again) and have it at your fingertips. This quick reference will save you a lot of worry. Maps are confusing when you are lost, in a hurry, or in a seething mass of people. When you look confused you become a perfect target for underground robbers, of which there are many. So before you start out, sit down with your agent or booker, or another model and plan the itineraries to and from your go-sees. Believe me, you will be glad you did. **Buses**: Tickets can be bought on the bus. You may also use one from a book of Metro tickets (carnet) or one of the various passes obtainable in the Métro. **Cars**: Vehicles drive on the right side of the street. If you do not have to drive in Paris, or anywhere else in Europe for that matter, don't. You will have enough problems and pressure without having to worry about hectic traffic conditions.

Currency: The unit of currency is the French franc (F or FF). One franc is equal to 100 centimes (ct).

Banks: Banks are the best places to change money. They are open on weekdays from 9:00 a.m.-4:30 p.m. Some banks are open later and on weekends. Always have your passport available when changing travelers checks.

Telephone: Paris numbers begin with a 4. Most phone boxes only take phonecards (telecartes) which can be bought at post offices or tobacconists. International calls or long-distance calls can be made from any post office. To call direct to the U.S.A. dial 19+1+area code+number. To make a collect call to the U.S.A. dial 19 (wait for the tone) 33 11 and wait for the operator to take the information. Parents calling Paris from the U.S. dial 011+33+1+number.

Postal Service: Post offices are open Monday-Friday 8:00 a.m.-7:00 p.m. and Saturday 8 a.m.-12 noon. The Bureau de Poste, at 52 rue du Louvre, is open twenty-four hours every day. Tel. 42 33 71 60. Postage stamps can be bought at a post office or tabac (tobacco shop), which also sells candy, film and souvenirs.

American Express: There are many branches but the most central is at 11 rue Scribe, near the famous Paris Opera House.

Embassy/Consulates: Canada: Embassy, 35av. Montaigne, 75008 Paris. Tel. 44 43 29 16; U.S.A: Embassy 2 avenue Gabriel, 75008 Paris. Tel. 42 96 12 02.

Toilets: Look for signs bearing the words DAMES (women) and MESSIEURS or HOMMES (both words mean men).

Time Difference: This is Greenwich Mean Time (GMT) plus one hour; Eastern Standard Time (EST) plus six hours; Daylight Saving Time is in effect from the end of March to the end of September.

Tipping: The term Service Compris means that the tip is included. This is the case in most hotels and restaurants; otherwise, the usual tip is 15 percent of the bill. Taxi tip is 15 percent. Gas station attendants and cinema and theater attendants should always be tipped.

Water: It is safe to drink unless you see a sign that reads, eau non potable. Most people drink bottled mineral water, which is inexpensive.

Electric Current: 220 volts AC in most places, although in the older buildings you will still find 110 volts. Make sure you have the necessary adapters. American appliances need a transformer.

Recommended Street Map: Plan de Paris

Police Emergency: Dial 17.

Milan

Models flock to Milan from all over the world. You really have the feeling that this is a model's city as you watch them rushing from one appointment to the next, or sipping cappuccino in the Piazza Duomo (site of the oldest and most beautiful Gothic cathedral in the world), exchanging ideas and news from home.

Milan has more international magazines than any other city. This means there is a lot of work. The competition, however, is enormous. The superstars are here and hundreds of other models of various levels of experience. In spite of this, Milan is an excellent market. A new model does not need tear sheets to get started; five or six good test pictures will do. In three months one can have a reasonable book and after six months, an excellent book, superb experience, beautiful tear sheets and prestige. A model who has "trained" in Milan can work anywhere. Not every agency has the time or inclination to develop new talent. A model who is accepted by one that does will be afforded the best possible start in the business.

There are three essentials for survival and success in Milan. First, you must have definite potential. This means excellent hair and figure, the right "look" for the market, a nice personality and a killer determination to succeed. The second essential is a reputable mother agent who knows the business inside and out on an international level and who has a strong liaison with and knows everything about, the Milan agency to which she is sending models. The third essential is that you are emotionally stable. If you are very insecure or have a dependency on drugs or alcohol do not go to Milan. In fact with these specific problems you shouldn't be in the profession at all, certainly not in Milan. The city is full of pretty, penniless young girls who call themselves models but who have had little or no experience. Most of them are trying to escape from broken homes and colorless backgrounds. The price of living la dolce vita is high. They fall prey to playboys who pick them up in chauffeur-driven limousines and shower them with furs and jewels—and drugs. This sad situation gives the profession and Milan, a bad reputation.

It is essential that you have health insurance and at least $1,500 to $2,000 in travelers checks.

Be aware that accommodation is a problem. Living conditions are sometimes shocking. Good apartments are scarce and expensive. Some agencies do have their own apartments or find pensiones or hotels to suit a new model's budget.

Milan can be glamorous and exciting. It is a fabulous city. The Milanese are warm and hardworking. Models are an accepted and welcome part of the Italian scene. If you are aware of the problems and it you are prepared to take your work seriously and learn from the experts of the modeling profession, you will have a fantastic time and gain confidence and the experience will be unbelievable.

There is runway, editorial, advertising and television commercial work here. Height for women is 5'9" and over with some exceptions. Men should be 6'0 and over. Weight and height must be in proportion. Agencies deduct thirty percent commission and twenty percent government tax, which can be reclaimed in the model's country of residence.

FASHION MODEL MANAGEMENT is one of the busiest and most prestigious agencies in the world and is one of the oldest in Europe. I interviewed Lorenzo Pedrini, one of the owners, at his plush agency. He explained that when Fashion takes a girl she will normally work within ten days. If she has not worked by the end of two or three weeks, she is sent home. "This rarely happens. Our girls generally work five days a week. If a girl has potential and a nice disposition she will work, make money and get a good book together. But if she doesn't have these basic requirements, I would advise her to change her career." I asked Lorenzo about the large number of would-be models in Milan who are broke and out of work. He told me: "The problems are not just in Milan. They are in every fashion city. The trouble is that these days everyone wants to start a model agency—in Milan, Paris, New York. Some of these people don't care about legalities. They don't arrange for work permits or pay the models properly. So, of course, there will be problems. It is the responsibility of the mother agent to check out the agents it is dealing with in foreign countries. She should know where she is sending the models. If a girl signs with a New York agent, she should be able to trust that agent completely. This is very important."

On the subject of the Milan nightclub and party scene, Lorenzo commented: "This agency is concerned with business. I try to stay out of the models' private lives. But if they ask for advice, I give it to them. But generally they will end up doing just the opposite of what I say."

I talked at length with agent Giampiero Paoletti. He told me: "An agency cannot have a specific look or style if it is going to provide as many moods as possible for the customer. An agency is a service. I also believe that if an agency wants to have strong management, it cannot have too many models. I love to find beautiful girls who are recognized as models immediately. But my challenge is to find interesting girls who are perhaps not so pretty but who have a great personality." Discussing the future of the industry, Giampiero said: "I believe there will be more beautiful girls, more cover girls. I don't see one model getting seven covers of Vogue, I see twelve different girls getting a cover every month."

One of my nicest experiences in Milan was an interview with Beatrice Traissac. Beatrice is a very caring person, much admired in the profession. Born in France, she has been in the modeling business in Milan for over twenty-five years. Her agency INTERNATIONAL BEATRICE MODELS has been one of the most successful in the world for over twenty years. Beatrice is always looking for new talent. She can spot potential "in a couple of seconds." She considers Milan to be the fashion capital of the world for a model.

"We have so many fine magazines here and the quality of tear sheets is good. A model does not require tear sheets to start out and she can have an excellent book at the end of six months that will enable her to work anywhere."

Beatrice considers lack of money and insurance the biggest problems for models in Milan. "So many times girls arrive without a penny. They ask us for help. We have to pay for rent, food and give them money just to get around Milan. They look on this agency as their second family—we can't see them in the streets. We should not be put in this situation. To come to Milan without money is a very serious mistake. A girl should have between $1,500 and $2,000, as well as health insurance, for her own peace of mind as well as her parents'. A man needs more money, because it will take him about two months to start working. Milan is primarily a woman's market.

If a girl arrives in Milan with a good book she will start immediately. Otherwise it will take a little longer. Anyone under fifteen years of age will not be accepted. We turn away a lot of fourteen-and-fifteen-year-olds even if they are beautiful and even if they are Italian, living close to home. They are too immature for this profession."

Beatrice and her staff are concerned about the welfare of their models in Milan. Each new model is briefed on agency rules and regulations, commission structure, the correct city map to buy and how to use the metro. Suitable apartments or pensions are arranged. "Milan is a wonderful experience for new models. It is a school, a training ground. They won't make great money here because the rates for work are not high. They will make enough money to get tear sheets and a good book—and that is why they are here.

"I warn parents to do a lot of investigating before they send their daughters to Europe. They must watch closely. I am a mother and that is what I would do."

Dr. Gianluca Causa, an expert on electronic imagery and transmission, had this to say: "Beginners must be prepared to stay at least three months to familiarize themselves with the market, the business and Milan. It takes two weeks to test and get a composite and it takes two months to promote the girls. We advance airfare if we are really sure of a girl's success and we provide apartments. This means that a model must cover her debts to the agency before she actually makes money."

Guiseppe and Patricia Piazzi, are a delightful husband and wife team who started the EYE FOR I agency in September 1991. In answer to a question about changes he had seen in the business over the past few years, Guiseppe said: "The pace is much faster now and so is the turnover of models. There is greater worldwide competition and this is good because it results in models being more professional and more qualified. This is better for clients, the magazines and the agencies."

Guiseppe has this advice for young men and women who are starting out in a modeling career: "Be strong. Don't give up. Be professional. Professionalism is very important. Learn about the business. Learn how to walk on a runway. Take photographic workshops. I urge mother agents and school directors to encourage new talent to do this."

I asked Bruno Pauletta, an international scout, what makes him decide to accept a girl and bring her to Milan. "It is eight years of being a booker becoming a scout. I know what the clients and the photographers want. I know this market from A to Z." Discussing the modeling scene today, he said: "There is not one kind of girl, not one look. The market requires brunettes, blondes, the very tall and sometimes even the very short." I asked Bruno about problems facing young girls in Milan. "Milan is a tough market to start at the bottom, especially for a girl from America who doesn't speak the language. She must be ready mentally to come here. If she is not, people will not work with her, even if she is the most beautiful girl in the world. They won't take the risk. My advice to girls who are not ready for Milan would be to first find another market in America—far away from family and friends, but still in America."

Marco Fabiano is one of the best agents for men in the world. He is immensely enthusiastic about his work and has a great eye for talent. He told me: "An agency has to be like a boutique. We have to be able to offer clients a variety of looks from classic to trendy. That is what they want. We can't have too many guys with similar looks." He added: "In Milan, magazines use only the best people. But we have a lot of magazines which makes it a good market for everyone. It also means that everyone must strive for excellence. It is hard for the beginner. There is so much strong competition. Everyone hears about the great tear sheets in Milan. It's not that easy."

Among other top agencies in this city are: FLASH MANAGEMENT GROUP (FOUR is the men's agency), ADMIRANDA MODEL AGENCY, ELITE and RICCARDO GAY MODEL MANAGEMENT

General City Information

Transportation: Airports: The two airports are Linate (for domestic and European flights) which is about six miles from the city center and Malpensa (for flights between continents), which is twenty-eight miles from town. A bus service every twenty minutes links both airports with the Stazione Centrale—the central station. **Taxis**: You can hail taxis in the street, but it is better to go to a taxi stand. You can also book one in advance. Taxis are yellow. Beware of any other type which is unmetered. The fare will be outrageous. This has happened to me when I have been in a hurry and jumped into the first one available. It is a good idea to establish the fare ahead of time. The fare will, however, differ from the fare on the meter if you have extra luggage or if you are traveling late at night. **Underground or Metro**: Look for the red sign with the letters MM on it. This stands for Metropolitana Milanese. There are three lines: the MM1, which is red; the MM2 which green; and the MM3 which is yellow. The subway is very easy to use and very inexpensive. Tickets are sold at newsstands in the station and must be stamped at the machine in the turnstile before you board a train. These newsstands close at 8:00p.m., or 1:00 p.m. on Sunday. You must have exact change to use ticket machines. Trains start at 6:20 a.m. and run until midnight. Special buses that follow the same route as the train run until 1:00 a.m. Bus, tram and subway tickets are interchangeable. Weekly passes are a very economical way to travel. They require a photograph which can be taken in a booth at a station. This must then be taken to the ticket office at the Duomo station where, after filling out the required forms, you will be given a travel pass. **Trams and Buses**: You may use subway tickets on trams and buses. There is no ticket conductor to sell tickets, so you may buy these at newsstands or at bars displaying a yellow sign bearing the words "Vendita Biglietti." Tickets may also be bought with exact change at ticket machines at some bus stops. These tickets are validated by punching them through a machine on the bus. There is a heavy fine if one is caught without a valid ticket. **Cars**: As in any city, cars are more of a problem than a convenience. If you do drive, stay on the right side of the road and be aware that there are rigid parking regulations in Milan.

Banks: Hours are 8:30 a.m.-1:30 p.m. and some reopen from 3:30 p.m.-4:30 p.m. They are closed on Saturday and Sunday.

Telephone: Phone cards are available at the SIP (Italian Telephone Service). You may make calls in restaurants or bars displaying a yellow telephone sign and pay for it at the cash register afterwards. Older telephones require tokens. To direct dial the United States use telephones labeled Teleselezione. The country code for Italy is 39;

the city code for Milan is 02. Dial 00+1+area code+number. Parents or friends calling Milan from the U.S. dial: 011+39+2(drop the 0)+ number. To place a call outside Italy, through an international operator, dial 15 and wait until you hear an operator. Be patient—this takes time! To call overseas dial 170. Again be prepared to wait for an operator. Tell him or her the number you are calling, then the number you are calling from. The operator will call you back when the connection has been made.

Postal Service: The main post office, the Posta Centrale, offers 24-hour service and is located in the Piazza Cordusio 1. It is closed on Sunday. Others are open 8:00 a.m.-2:00 p.m. weekdays and Saturday from 8:00a.m.-2:00 p.m.

Embassies/Consulates: Canada: 19 via Vittor Pisani, Milan. Tel. 02 6697451; U.S.A.: 10 via Principe Amedeo 2, Milan. Tel. 02 290351.

Tipping: A service and a cover charge will be added to your bill. Take these extra charges into account if you are short of money. If you are feeling rich and have had excellent service in a good restaurant, an extra 10 percent gratuity will be appreciated. Keep your receipts—you can be fined for leaving a restaurant without one!

Water: The water is generally safe to drink. In pensiones it is wise to ask first. If you are a newcomer it is probably better to drink bottled water.

Electric Current: 220 volts, AC

Recommended Street Map: There are several good maps of Milan. Be sure to buy one with bus, tram and subway routes.

Toilet: Look for the W.C. sign. You can also ask for the toilette, or say, "Dove sta il gabinetto?" which means, "Where is the toilet?"

Time Difference: Greenwich Mean Time + 1, Eastern Standard Time + 6, Daylight Saving Time is April-September.

Police Emergency: Dial 113.

Madrid and Barcelona

Spain has become a very important country for all business, including modeling. There is work for new and experienced models. The standard is high and the competition is strong. Beginners have to be good.

The look for men is tall (minimum 6'1"), masculine and healthy. Women must be at least 5'8½" tall, slim and have a fresh, natural look. Models with acting ability do very well thanks to the large television commercial industry. All of the agents to whom I spoke agreed that models must have a good personality, a strong sense of discipline and be extremely professional. The A.M.E. (Association de Modelos de Espana), is the modeling association of Spain. It protects models' rights and controls fees.

One agent and international scout gave me this advice for new American models: "Be emotionally prepared to work in different environments, with different people who have different working methods. The market in Europe is not the same as in the United States, so be prepared to change your look. Learn about Spain—the lifestyle and customs—before you come."

Madrid is the center of the fashion industry. There is a lot of editorial work making it an ideal place for tear sheets. GROUP INTERNATIONAL scouts a lot around the world for men and women to do high fashion and some television work.

Barcelona is the catalog capital and fashion here is more avant-garde. The television commercial industry is big. The market is very commercial. It is not the place for tear sheets. It is a good market for beginners.

I talked with Joseph (Pepe) Julia who has been a tax collector for twenty years. He described this job as "very boring" and told me he had always wanted to own a model agency. He knew very little about the procedure until he met two former models who shared his ambition. In 1996 they opened FLEMING MODELS which today is one of the most successful agencies in Spain. Joseph looks for tall, blonde girls with a "California look". Height must be 5'8" to 6'. Age range is 16-21. Discussing the type of work in Barcelona, Joseph said: "In January and February there is a lot of runway. The rest of the year there is catalog and television commercials. Barcelona is famous for its production work."

NATASHA'S MODELS is the oldest agency in Spain and represents men and women.

There are other agencies in Madrid and Barcelona that represent all types of work and have strong liaisons with agencies around the world.

Scandinavia

Norway, Sweden and Denmark produce beautiful models. These countries are regular scouting grounds for model agents.

Sighsten Herrgardh, a Stockholm journalist, pioneered the business in Scandinavia when he opened the STOCKHOLM GRUPPEN AGENCY in Sweden years ago. In February 1989 John Casablancas swung Scandinavia into the international spotlight when he opened ELITE COPENHAGEN in Denmark. His expertise in model management had a great impact.

As most Scandinavians are blond and blue-eyed, models with dark hair, brown eyes and a slightly exotic look are in demand. American men do well. For them, their "look"—which can be either rugged and masculine or have a boyish cast—is more important than their age. Height for men is 6'0" to 6'2"; for women it is 5'8" and over.

Norway, Sweden and Denmark are excellent markets for local models who commute between countries. Americans are usually brought in for pre-booked assignments.

I met agent Susanne Östling while she was scouting in America. She was impressed with the modeling school system here. She said: "In Sweden there is no chance to learn modeling. At my agency I train the girls myself and then send them to Greece and Milan to build up their books. Sweden is a good place to start a career. It's a difficult market but a nice experience. However, a model will never become rich here." Discussing the differences in the approach to modeling in the two countries, Susanne told me: "In Sweden modeling is not looked at as a profession. It is something that is done between jobs. It is not the be-all and end-all. After you become a model, you invest your money or go on to be a doctor or a lawyer. Swedish people want to become models for the traveling and the money. In America these things are important, but to become a model— that is what is really important."

Norway is smaller than Sweden and most of the agencies are in Oslo. Denmark is a bigger market than Norway or Sweden and models make more money here.

Among the top agencies: In Sweden: CHIC MODEL AGENCY, VASTVENSKA MODELLGRUPPEN, MIKAS, AVENUE MODELLER and SCANDINAVIAN MODELLINK. In Norway: TEAM MODEL & STYLIST MANAGEMENT, KRISTIJ MANNEQUINER & FOTOMODELLER and PRESTIGE MODEL AGENCY. In Denmark: FASHION TEAM, SCANDI-NAVIAN MODELS APS/ELITE and UNIQUE MODELS (both in Copenhagen). There are other successful agencies in this city.

Austria and Finland

Vienna, Austria, has a small specific market. The work is mostly advertising but clients prefer models with an editorial look for their campaigns. It is ideal for French or other European girls who do not want to travel or work far from home. The pay is not very good. It is not a market for American models except for specific assignments or for gaining experience in a very beautiful city.

There are nine agencies in Vienna. Among them are ELITE, NEXT COMPANY MODEL MANAGEMENT, STELLA MODELS & TALENT and

VANITY FAIR.

I had not planned to include Finland in this book until I had the pleasure of interviewing Liisa Kangas-Hauta-aho, the president of the PARISS MODEL AGENCY and MODELING SCHOOL in Seinajoki and Helsinki. Liisa organizes the Model of Finland competition held annually in November. She told me that modeling is becoming increasingly popular in Finland. Her models work all over the country and through her excellent international connections with agencies, all over the world. The European Union (EU) has created excellent networking opportunities for agents and more job opportunities for models.

Female models must be at least 5'9" and aged between 16 and 22. Men must be a minimum of 6' and aged 18 or over. The agency arranges accommodation. English is the second language in Finland therefore communication is not a problem for Americans.

Another excellent agency is SUOMEN EUROPE FASHION.

Athens

A number of young models I met during my travels urged me "to check out Greece" as a launching pad for a career. I needed little persuasion. I love this country have spent many summer holidays on the island of Mykonos. In Athens I found successful agencies.

Mary Dracopoulou owns MODELS ONE. A former Miss Greece, Mary is a pioneer of the industry here. As a former international model and with an extensive background in advertising, marketing and public relations, Mary is a true ambassador of fashion for her country. She is largely responsible for the high standard of professionalism among agents, models, photographers, clients and others in the industry. She told me: "This market has been developing rapidly over the last few years. We have a lot of great magazines and our editorials are tremendous. We attract top models and photographers and the standard is high. It is less competitive than Paris and Milan or any other European market. For the right models, things happen quickly. The people are friendly, the clients are nice, the weather is beautiful and it is safe."

Mary told me that Greece has more commercial productions than major European markets. The quality of television commercials is very high. With over twenty private and three major television channels there is a lot of work in this medium. MODELS ONE represents men aged eighteen and over who are 6' tall (minimum). Height requirement for women starts at 5'9" and the age range is

16-21. Personality and character are also main considerations. This agency has divisions for children and actors and handles direct bookings for international celebrities.

Vivi Christi, an agent and international scout, told me: "Models can get excellent tear sheets here. Athens is a small good market for new faces. Even if models have only two or three pictures in their books, that is enough. They don't need a lot of money to live here. Athens is safe, has a lovely night life and very interesting people."

ACE MODELS, ACTION!, FASHION CULT, MODEL'S HOUSE LTD., PRESTIGE GROUP and TWINS MODELS AGENCY are hardworking, successful, reputable agencies.

The Asian Market

The Asian market has opened up considerably in recent years and this has increased opportunities for male and female models. Tokyo and Osaka in Japan used to be the only cities for work. Now models are happy to travel to Taipei in Taiwan and to Seoul in Korea. I interviewed many agents in these markets and was particularly impressed with the concern they all had for the welfare of their models. At every reputable agency owners and staff are honest and fair about what they can do for the model and what is expected in return. I strongly advise any model with plans to go there to study the culture in advance.

Tokyo

Tokyo is a teeming mass of people, buildings and traffic. The words traffic jam have no meaning until experienced in this city! Despite the crush and frenzied pace, there is law, order and tremendous gentility here. Young people jump at the opportunity to speak English. Everyone is very helpful.

There is editorial, commercial print, television commercial and runway work for men and women. For the Tokyo Collections in April and November and the big September fashion shows, models must be at least 5'9"(women) and 6'0"(men). Experienced models with good portfolios do extremely well. New models learn the business and have the experience of a lifetime. If they do not make money the first time, they will not be out of pocket. And the education is priceless.

Almost every model who has worked in Japan raves about it. A few have been disillusioned having lacked the stamina for the demanding pace. One young American model was relieved when the time came to return to the United

States. She was exhausted after her stay in Tokyo and found that the financial rewards were not worth the endless strain and pressure. Agents point out that some models have incorrect preconceived ideas. It sounds tempting when you hear that all models are admitted to night clubs free of charge and that all drinks are free, but some models have abused this resulting in the demise of their careers. In Japan, more than anywhere else, if a model does not play by the rules and does not look and behave professionally, his or her career will end quickly. The penalty for being caught with one joint of marijuana is three months in jail and deportation.

The work routine is the same as in other countries, but the model agency system is different. There are specific rules, regulations and requirements. Government law requires that there be a standard, guaranteed, exclusive sixty-day contract between model agency and foreign model. The government also requires that agencies guarantee the following: a minimum amount of earnings for that period regardless of whether the model works or not, a prepaid round-trip airfare ticket and accommodation.

Japanese model agencies take 20 percent commission and withhold an obligatory 20 percent for taxes. They do not use a voucher system, so a model should keep a record of money earned. There are no set fees for work and bookers negotiate with clients. Payment is made at the end of the contract, before the model leaves Japan. In the meantime, the agency will advance an adequate living allowance. Keep in mind that the cost of living is very high.

Sandi Bass is a scout for AGENCE PRESSE MODEL MANAGEMENT, one of the top agencies in Tokyo. Sandi is an authority on modeling in Japan having lived and modeled there for five years. For ten years before that, she was a top model in Europe. Sandi generously gave me this information: "I travel worldwide scouting models at the top agencies. I also go to small agencies in small cities –you never know where you will find the next face of the moment. We offer contracts, therefore I have to feel sure that the model will work and still there are no guarantees. This makes my job very difficult.

"The requirements for Tokyo are specific. Height 5'6" to 5'10½", good body measurements (34-24-34 is ideal), good skin, good personality, an interesting face and a good portfolio. At Agence Presse we require a model to have at least ten to twelve good editorial shots in her portfolio. Tear sheets are a definite plus. The clients want to see that the model has worked and how he or she photograph. The stronger the model, the stronger the pay. Models must have a positive, pleasant attitude. The hours are long and even though the clients try to make the working conditions as comfortable as possible some models still complain. Patience and professionalism are very important."

MODEL CHIC president, Tsutomu Oki, explained the government's agency contract rule: "The government does not want us to bring in anyone who will not work. This protects the model from unemployment. The guarantee will pay back what they owe for airfare, apartments and other expenses. However, if we offer someone ten thousand dollars we believe that they are going to book twenty or fifty thousand dollars and more. At Chic we only take models who will meet the qualifications of the Japanese market, not just the people who have the qualifications to be a model." This agency represents men and women.

Yoshura Furuya has been in the business for over twenty-five years and has owned her own agency, YOSHIE, INC., for most of that time. She emphasized how the market has changed, that there are fewer jobs and that there is less money to be made. "An agency must be very sure that a model will work," she said. Age range for her agency is sixteen to twenty-four; height 5'7" (5'6" in some cases) to 5'9".

WORLD TOP MODEL is quite a small agency for men and women. Owner Hiromi Tashiro believes in personal individual attention. She is very down-to-earth and realistic about the situation for models in Japan. "Some girls think that if they are chosen to come to Japan they will make a lot of money. This is not necessarily so. But we do everything possible to make their stay a success. If a girl likes it in Japan, she wants to come back over and over again." Hiromi stressed the importance of correct body measurements, especially the hip size of 35" (maximum). "School directors and model agents in America must keep their promise when they say that a girl has the specific measurements. "Models can not come here and then start to lose weight."

Thomas Gusway who co-owns agencies in British Columbia and Los Angeles was most anxious to set the record straight for everyone involved in modeling in Japan. He explained the visa requirements: "First of all the agent in Japan has to apply to the government for a visa certificate. This is sent to the "mother agent" in America who must send it to the nearest Consulate for approval. The 90-day visa which is issued can be renewed in Japan for another 90 days after which the model must leave the country and start the process all over again." On the subject of contracts and guarantees he said: "My philosophy is there are no guarantees in life except death and taxes. Every contract has some clause that can be broken. If someone guarantees you something, they expect you to perform. If you are not going to perform to a certain point, they must have clauses to protect themselves. If you do what you are supposed to do and behave the way you are supposed to behave and it doesn't work out as everyone had hoped, the Japanese agency is saying that they will make sure you are not in a dire situation." Tom has many models working successfully in the Asian market.

There are many excellent agencies in Tokyo. Among them are: AD-PLAN TOKYO, TEAM, BRAVO, KIRARA, ELITE, FOLIO and FRIDAY MODEL AGENCY.

General City Information

I have been to Japan many times and can assure you that your stay there will be enjoyable and educational. Your agency will guide and help you. I have added this information section to show you that Tokyo, which is the center of the modeling profession in Japan, has basically the same services as any other major city. Although there is a great change in language and culture, if you read this section before you go, you will be enlightened, more confident and when you arrive, home will not seem so far away.

Transportation: Airport: There are two airports, the New Tokyo International Airport which is still called by its old name, Narito, and Hanedo Airport, which handles domestic flights. There are many bus and train services in to the city center and the journey takes about ninety minutes. Taxis for this ride are prohibitively expensive. I strongly advise you to confirm that you will be met by an agency representative. **Taxis**: Taxis show a red light in the bottom left corner of the windshield when they are available. Passenger doors open by remote control so stand clear when the car pulls up. Meters record the exact fare and tipping is not expected. Taxis are hard to get and they are more expensive after midnight, when all public transport closes down. **Subways and Trains**: Tokyo's mass transit system is fast and efficient. Names of stations are written in English and Japanese. You can ask for information in English at information desks at certain stations. As in every big city, avoid rush-hour crowds. All public transport closes down at midnight. **Buses**: The extensive bus service is complicated to use and to understand. Before you use the system learn it from someone who is familiar with it. **Cars**: Traffic is fast and furious and drives on the left side of the street.
Currency: The monetary unit is the Japanese yen (Y). Learn the currency ahead of time and this will be one thing less to cope with when you arrive. Check the rate of exchange in advance.
Banks: Open weekdays 9:00 a.m.-3:00 p.m.
Telephone: Four colors differentiate the use of public telephones. The yellow,

green, purple and gray phones accept Y10 and Y100 coins. Green and gray phones accept telephone cards. Make international calls from gray phones. Tokyo's area code is 03. The country code is 81. To direct dial a number in the U.S., the sequence is 001+area code+ number of party. To call Tokyo from the U.S., dial 011+81+3 (drop the 0 from the 03 area code) +number.

Postal Service: Weekdays: 9:00 a.m.-5:00 p.m., Sat. 9:00 a.m.-12-30 a.m. The Central Post Office is located at 2-7-2 Marunouchi, Chiyoda-ku. Hours are Mon.-Fri. 9 a.m.-7p.m., Sat. 9 a.m.-5 p.m., Sun. and public holidays, 9 a.m.-12:30 p.m.

American Express: American Express International: Located in the Yurakucho Denki Bldg., 1-7-1 Yurakucho, Chiyoda-ku. Tel. 03/3214-0280

Embassies/Consulates: U.S.A.: 1-10-5 Akasaka, Minato-ku, Tokyo. Tel. 03/3224 5000; Canada: 7-3-38 Akasaka, Minato-ku, Tokyo. Tel. 03/3408 2101

Toilet: Look for W.C. signs.

Time Difference: Japan is nine hours ahead of Greenwich Mean Time (GMT) and there is no Daylight Saving Time. The time difference can be really confusing. For instance, when you fly from Tokyo to Los Angeles you cross the International Date Line and arrive in Los Angeles hours before you left Tokyo— you actually gain a day.

Water: You may drink the water unless otherwise informed

Electric Current: 100 volts, AC

Language: Some English is spoken. If you speak slowly, people will try to understand and respond.

Police Emergency: Dial 110 for police and 119 for fire or ambulance. Speak slowly. No money is required at a public phone—just push the red button before dialing.

Osaka

This market is predominantly for catalog work. The 5'7" model will work here. There are good agencies in this city, namely: COSMOPOLITAN, FORZA INC., SELECT MEN MODEL MANAGEMENT, VISAGE and ZEM, INC.

Seoul, Korea

The Korean market is comparatively new and is growing. It has mostly catalog work but there is some editorial, advertising and film work. Agents like the clean, fresh, girl-next-door look. Age range is 14-22. Height 5'8"-5'9". Body measurements must be 34-24-34. Height require-

ment for men is 6'-6'1". Jacket size, 40R.

Korea's top designers take their collections to Paris, Milan and New York. They like to use American models.

The cost of living is cheaper here than in Japan. Food and taxis are very inexpensive. Rent for a model's apartment in Seoul is $400-$500 a month compared to $1400-$1600 in Tokyo.

Sunny Chae is a former school director who owns the WHAT'S NEW INC. agencies in Seattle and Seoul. She has first hand knowledge of the market and prepares young men and women for work in Korea. I asked her about monetary guarantees and other requirements. She said: "We don't have test photographers in Korea so models must have a good portfolio and composites before they go. We guarantee a certain amount of money depending on the model's experience and the number of tear sheets she has. For two months that guarantee ranges from $8,000 to $18,000."

She had this advice for agencies and school directors planning to send models to Korea: "Be careful of the agent you are dealing with there. Make sure they are licensed and have a good reputation. Also, in Korea there is no minimum age for buying cigarettes or alcohol. If you feel a girl cannot avoid these temptations, don't send her. At my agency we have a chaperone to take girls to and from go-sees. I am overly protective of my models but I am also overly picky of the type I select. I find that girls who have a problem at home or in school, usually have a problem in this business."

Koreans learn English in second and third grades. In high school they must study French, German and Japanese. While language is not a problem, niceties are lost in translation. Sunny mentioned a couple of cultural differences which can cause shock. She told me: "While Korean people can speak, read and write English, they sometimes lack communication skills. For instance, if they are concerned about a girl who is gaining weight, they might say, 'You are fat.' instead of saying 'You must watch your diet because you are gaining weight.' This hurts the model's sensitivity. I ask the girls not to take this sort of thing personally and to make allowances for the language differences. In Korea 13 and 14-year-olds look like kids and we pat them on the butt or on the shoulder. American girls of this age look more mature. I tell Korean agents they can't do that to American girls because they might think it is sexual harassment. I have heard this said several times."

Other successful agents in this city are: STARS AGENCY, INC.,

CLASSY INT'L MODEL MANAGEMENT, SEOUL MODELS, INC. and SUN INT'L MODEL MANAGEMENT.

Taiwan

Taipei is the capital city. I was very impressed by the diligence with which agents here do business. As with all reputable Asian agents, they are intense and specific and very anxious that agents and school directors in America understand how the industry works in the Orient.

This is not an expensive city. Height requirement for women is 5'7" to 5'9" and for men, 5'11" to 6'1". The agency in Taiwan obtains the necessary visa. The government then grants the working permit. One agent told me: "Yes, we guarantee a certain amount of money. The amount depends on the experience of the model. She will never be out of pocket because if she doesn't make money, she doesn't have to pay us back." But agents here have a good eye. When we take girls, we know they will work."

There are excellent agencies in Taipei including: COSMOPOLITAN MODEL AGENCY, FMI-FACE MODELS INT'L, FASHION MODEL MANAGEMENT, MODE MODELS, NEW FACE MODEL AGENCY and UNIQUE MODEL MANAGEMENT.

South Africa

South Africa has two centers for modeling. Johannesburg is one of the markets and there is catalogue, advertising, television and television commercial work here. The fun place to be, however, is Capetown an incredibly beautiful spot with fabulous beaches, mountains, climate and nightlife.

There are first rate agencies here as well as high caliber magazines such as Elle, Marie Claire and Cosmopolitan. Editorial models with strong portfolios get excellent tear sheets and catalog models do extremely well. Television commercials are produced for the international market. Peak months are September-May. Age range for girls is 14-21 and for men, 17 and over.

Agencies in this city include: ASHWIN MODEL MANAGEMENT, NEXT MANAGEMENT, HEADS MODEL AGENCY and the G3 MODEL AGENCY PTY LTD.

Brazil

Sao Paolo is the center of the fashion industry in this city of sunshine, samba, jazz and golden beaches. Everyone takes time to enjoy life. There are terrific opportunities for tear sheets but the history of inflationary money problems does not make Brazil the ideal place for high earnings.

An American agent who closed his agency in Rio de Janeiro told me: "Brazil is not established with its own models. Clients fly in models from abroad. It has beautiful scenery, excellent photographers and its own issues of Harper's Bazaar, Vogue, Elle and Chinese Elle. A model can have tear sheets within a month and a complete portfolio suitable for the New York market within two months. This is not a money market, however, because of the strong inflation rate."

Australia

Australia ranks third for model earnings in the world. Japanese clients shoot big campaigns here and at least fifteen high fashion magazines are published in Sydney. Fares to Australia from the United States and Europe are expensive; consequently, agents have to be certain that the models they accept have the qualifications that will enable them to earn at least sufficient money to pay back advanced expenses.

Sydney is the center of fashion and advertising and is, therefore, the city for print work. Melbourne is the place for catalog work. Models can make money in both cities. If they have tear sheets and obvious potential, agents will advance airfare. Otherwise models must pay expenses.

The 'look' in Australia tends to reflect the 'look' in Europe. Height requirement for women is 5'8" to 5'10; for men it is 5'11" to 6'0". The blond, tanned, energetic, muscular male is in demand.

Gordon Charles who owns PLATFORM MODELS in Sydney, is extremely charming and knowledgeable about the business worldwide. He has over thirty years experience ten of which were spent as an international model. His agency has affiliates in Melbourne and Brisbane. We discussed the industry in Australia. He said: "We are primarily a summer market. The models with good bodies and good skin texture make the real money. There is a lot of editorial work and opportunities for tear sheets. The rate for editorial is $150 U.S. Of course no one does editorial to make money anywhere in the world. They do it for the kudos and the credibility."

Gordon firmly believes that potential models who are educated about the business stand a much better chance for a successful career. His agency has a development program for new girls aged between 14-18. "Once a girl gets past 18 it is too competitive on a global level for her to start learning the ropes." Gordon advises American girls who want to discover the Australian market to do so during their summer vacation for a minimum of three months. "At my agency we develop them at this time and then they can come back to work and go on to other markets. Apart from airfare, they will need between $2000-$3000 to pay for testing, photographs and living expenses." The agency has apartments at famous Bondi Beach.

Longtime agent Peter Chadwick told me: "Australia has become a very popular market. First of all we have world-class magazines and superb photographers. The weather is terrific. Models love it here, especially the guys who take their surfboards to the beach as soon as they have finished a shoot. And clients like to work here because of a combination of these things."

Vivien Smith is well known and highly respected in modeling circles around the world. She is responsible for bringing modeling in Australia up to international standards. Vivien opened an agency in Sydney in 1966 and agencies in Melbourne and Brisbane followed. Judy Steeves, a scout told me: "Australia has a very high standard of modeling. At VIVIEN'S we really only bring in top girls. We are interested in girls who want to build up their books if they are really stunning." A young American makeup artist and hair stylist, who spent three months with this agency told me: "Australia is a booming market. Everyone wants to go there—clients, film people and models. There is a lot of work and there is not the pressure of other big cities. Everyone is laid-back. They all work together, but they are not in a mad rush. People are friendly and really enjoy life. I loved working in Australia."

There are several things, apart from the great amount of work, that account for the Australian market's popularity. Australia is an excellent place to get tear sheets and put together a portfolio. For most models, there is no language barrier. Australia is a safe place to work and live. The people are friendly, easygoing and sincere and the country and climate are beautiful. Note that the seasons are reversed—it is midsummer in December. I remember spending one Christmas Day sizzling in the sun on

Sydney's Bondi Beach. I spent a great deal of time in Australia and I also lived in the Earl's Court (dubbed "Kangaroo Valley" because of the number of Australian residents) and Kensington areas of London, where many of my friends and neighbors were "Aussies." They are super people. If you get a chance to work "down under" (Australia is often called that because of its location—south of the equator), then good on you, Sheila (or mite). It's a beaut! And that's fair dinkum! (That's Australian for "good for you, girl –or mate." If you get the chance, take it. It is great and that's the truth!)

Other excellent agencies in Sydney are: CAMERON'S, TOP MODELGROUP, PAMELA'S and MCTV MODEL MANAGEMENT. In the Melbourne area there are several agencies, including another branch of CAMERON'S and COSMOPOLITAN MODEL MANAGEMENT.

General Information
Metric: Australia uses the metric system of weights and measures. Temperatures are measured in Celsius (centigrade).
Currency: The dollar is the monetary unit. One dollar equals 100 cents.
Banks: Hours are 9:30 a.m.-4:00 p.m. Monday through Friday.
Telephone: Australia has a sophisticated system. International access code is 011, country code is 61; city code for Sydney is 2 and for Melbourne it is 3.
Postal Service: Post office hours are 9:00 a.m.-5:00 p.m. Monday through Friday.
Electric Current: The electric current is 240/250 volts, AC. You will no doubt need a voltage converter and an adapter for the three-pin pub outlets.

Sydney
Sydney is the capital of the State of New South Wales.

General Information
Transportation: Airport: The airport is located about six miles from the center of the city. The bus or taxi trip takes about thirty minutes.
Climate: Summer months are November to March. Days are sunny and hot and nights are mild. Winter months are June to August. At this time it is cool and rainy, but there are a lot of sunny days. Nights are cold. These conditions apply to Melbourne also.

Chapter 9

Children

I have watched many casting directors and model agents judge child actors and models at competitions and conventions. I have attended many casting sessions. I have interviewed some of the best children's agents and casting directors in the world. This chapter will tell you what they are looking for, how to get your child into the business successfully and how to avoid spending thousands of dollars.

The child who is natural, polite, well-disciplined and who can follow directions is at a great advantage. A child who pouts and refuses to do what he or she is told at home will probably behave the same way with a casting director or a model agent—but only once.

Many children are either too shy or too outgoing when confronted by an agent or a camera. The child who gets the job is somewhere in between.

Careers must be supervised very closely. Children should never be dropped off at a photographic shoot or casting. If they don't get a job, be light-hearted about it; rejection isn't easy at any age. If they are successful, try to take it in your stride without too much attention—this will take away the pressure of having to be successful next time.

As the mother of a child who did several national television commercials during grade and junior school, I am aware that taking a child out of school for an audition, is a difficult decision if it happens very often. It is very stressful for a child who is a cheerleader or a member of a baseball or swim team to miss a game or practice to answer the call of showbiz. They are torn between team spirit and school commitment and the glamour of being in a television commercial. And let's face it, the money earned on television beats cutting the neighborhood lawns for pocket money any day!

It is up to the parent to keep a good balance. A legitimate casting for a national commercial could result in a major contribution to college tuition and is certainly worth the time.

To start your child in the business you need a couple of Polaroid pictures: a smiling head shot (don't worry if a tooth is missing—it could be a $100,000 gap!) and a full-length shot in a favorite outfit. A little boy with tousled hair, shorts, sneakers, T-shirt and a toothy grin will have the edge over a boy in a suit, tie and sleek hairdo, unless this is what is called for. Send the pictures to a local agent. If the agent is interested, you may be asked to have a few professional shots taken. A representative of the COLLEEN CLER AGENCY, representing 400 children, in Burbank, California, said: "The agents know what the clients are looking for, the parents do not. The agents know what type of pictures is needed. No one should spend more that $400 on these."

Never spend money on a portfolio for a baby or a young child. In three months they will look different. The pictures in your wallet will do just fine.

Here is another tip. If the children are taking part in a runway competition, don't try to teach them how to walk and turn like professional adult models. And don't dress them up in starchy outfits they have never worn before and will never wear again. Let them be natural and dress them in something attractive and comfortable. Allow children to be children—on the runway, in front of the camera, or onstage.

I asked one New York agent to compare a child model's professional life with that of an adult. She said: "With the exception of rejection, which is the same for both age groups, one of our biggest problems is having to deal with parents who want the business more than their child does. It is what they wanted to do when they were young. Children should never be made to feel that getting a certain commercial or print job is a matter of life or death. It should be fun for them and when it ceases to be fun, they should be out of the business."

Jeff Morrone, an energetic, enthusiastic and charming young man, had specific information and advice for parents and children. "The quickest way to determine if a child doesn't have the desire to be in the business is if he cries when he knows he has an audition, or if she fusses and has to be taken out to eat and coaxed to go. This usually means that the desire is the parents' and I would tell these parents to back off."

Another children's agent told me: " A third of the market now is children. I look for boys and girls with lots of energy, ranging in age from four to eighteen. The best way for parents to get their kids started is to send snapshots to an agent and include a stamped, self-addressed envelope. If they are interested, someone from the agency will follow up with a phone call. I would advise parents who are looking for an agent to make sure the agency does not have too many children—especially of the age of their child. Parents want to be sure that their child will get private attention and lots of exposure."

I found the people who are responsible for building children's careers to be extremely caring. Two such people, Coretha Timko and Michael Harrah, who own CMT Management/JLO West, are personal managers in Los Angeles. They consult and direct workshops for young adults and children. Coretha had this to say: "One of the things we gripe about is girls trying to look older than they are when the business wants them to look as young as possible. Sometimes a parent will call us and say they have an extremely talented teenage daughter who looks very young. We ask them to bring her in emphasizing that she must look as young as possible. When the child comes in she's wearing blush, mascara, lipstick and a hairstyle that is unbelievable. It's hilarious!" Coretha also emphasized how important it is that the child desire the career. She said: "When we talk with them one on one, without a parent around, we know if it is something they are excited about."

Michael had this to say: "There are opportunities for children we never dreamed of ten years ago. The whole market is expanding and we are returning to family entertainment. We are looking for boys and girls who look like real boys and girls; who don't have a slickness to them that prevents them from being believable as the kid next door, or the bad boy in class, or the street kid that has had to grow up on his own. The child must want to do this with a vengeance and the parent must be supportive. It is going to be a huge commitment not only for the child or parent but also for any other family member involved. It changes your life completely." Coretha added: "We are interested in personality as well as looks. Sometimes a dynamite four-year-old becomes introverted at six. You would be surprised how often that happens."

Los Angeles casting director Clair Sinnett is a professor in the drama department at the University of California, Irvine. Clair's impressive career has been constant since high school. She has excelled as an actor, casting director, producer, singer, dancer, director, agent and coach. I asked Clair for advice for parents. She said: "If this is something the child wants to do, they will do it well. We have to protect their spontaneity and creativity and not make them into miniature adults. When children go to an audition they need to say the lines the way they would say them as opposed to parents giving them line readings. When parents do this the children end up like 30-year-old midgets! Children have to be very fresh and look like kids—as if they had just come from school or the playground."

Judy Savage started her thirty-year career in show business as stage mother and manager to her three talented children, Mark, Tracie and Brad. All three had very successful careers in television, films and theatre as well as appearing in television commercials. Then they went to college and into related fields of the entertainment industry. By this time, Judy was "addicted" to building children's careers. For this purpose she opened The Judy Savage Agency in Hollywood. In over 20 years she has had phenomenal success. "Last year I had thirty children appearing in television series and twenty-five in movies." She credits much of this success to finding acting classes taught by Diane Hardin whose Young Actors Space school has wide recognition in the industry. "When I was looking for acting classes for my own children, I visited sixty different facilities before I found the Young Actors Space. I sat there and cried through a whole acting class. I knew this was it. This was real work."

Discussing the need for education in this field, Judy said: "The acting in films today is so much more real than it was thirty years ago. The style has changed. Shirley Temple was a brilliant little performer but you couldn't sell a little performer like that today. It is not real. So much more is expected of the young actor. Considering the money producers are risking on movies today, they have to have people that are good. Training is a necessity."

I asked Judy at what age a child should be considered ready for instruction. She explained: "When they are small they should be natural. Their own spontaneity is all they need. They can get by being cute. Even things like a lisp are fine. By the time they are eight, no one wants that anymore. I generally wait until a child can read, which is somewhere around six to eight depending on the child." She added: "Most of the children who are successful are very bright. It's almost genetic. They are little performers from the time they are born. When they walk into my office they just glow. I can spot the desire in a second."

I asked Judy for advice for parents in small towns whose children want to get into the business. She said: "Bloom where you are planted. There is sure to be church, community and school theatre. Do everything you can in your area before you come to Los Angeles. Even for people who live here who have the look, the size, the personality, the passion and the intelligence, it still takes about three years before something good happens. The average length of a career in Hollywood is five years. The number of people who actually earn a living is one percent. An adult actor may go three or four years without a job. You can imagine the highs and lows of that. It is like Vegas. It is a total gamble. That is why I preach to every single child that comes into my office to go to college. When you are accepted into college you can postpone going for a year or two – but go! You have got to have something to fall back on.

"This is a great career for kids because they can get it out of their system. They can pay for their braces, their caps, their cars and their college and then they can move on. Very few make the transition to adult actors. But a lot of ex-child actors are directors or producers or are in some other aspect of the business. It is definitely addictive. Once you are in it any other kind of business seems boring."

Chapter
10

Specialty Modeling

Large or Plus Sizes

This market has an interesting background. In the mid-seventies, big changes took place in certain areas of the fashion industry. The junior, or teenage, market had started to decline and the predictions were that it would continue to do so, even more rapidly. Initial studies showed that teenagers who had been born during the baby boom era and who had romped through their teenage years on a compulsive multibillion-dollar spending spree were now in or nearing their thirties, where marriage, motherhood and budgets would leave them less money to spend on clothes. (Statistics show that a woman starting a family spends much less money on clothes than a teenager.) As the baby boom had been followed by a period of zero population growth, there would be fewer teenagers to buy clothes and, therefore, that particular market would drop off.

Meanwhile there was a new category of clothes buyer in the store— the career woman. Studies showed that a working woman who earned $10,000 a year spent more on clothes than the wife of an executive who earned $50,000. However, although there was a noticeable growth in the career market, there was little hope that this would make up the deficit in teenage spending. Additional in-depth studies were done in New York in an effort to find other markets that would recapture the American dollar. One bombshell dropped by the study was that the fashion industry, which had always assumed that fashion-conscious women loved to diet and were rich enough to go to "fat farms" to stay trim, had been wrong. The shocking revelation was that 30 percent of American women wore a size 16 or over. Of these women, five to seven million were large-size women with moderate to high incomes, fourteen million had moderate incomes and six to seven million were budget customers. The fashion industry was ecstatic. Here was the answer to the drop in teenage buying—an untapped and very lucrative large-size market. It is interesting to note that a top designer, who was ready to retire, was asked to put her name on a large-size boutique line of clothing, she declined, stating that large sizes were not her image. Today, that same designer says, "That snobbery was the biggest mistake I ever made. I could have ended my career in a blaze of glory as a pioneer and trendsetter instead of ending it as just another talented designer. I didn't do it because I was a snob. I didn't know what the large-size woman looked like. In fact, she is beautiful and there are so many of her."

Manufacturers responded to the fashion-industry study by producing cute and elegant clothes to fit larger sizes. There was still a problem, however. Buyers balked, saying their customers would not look right in them. There had to be a way to show that these designs would look good on large women. A large-size model was found and then another. The solution was a success. Buyers bought the clothes and a new category of model was suddenly in demand.

Mary Duffy is a dynamic, vivacious New Yorker whose modeling career began in Boston, where she ran an art gallery and modeled large-size clothes on the side. Mary was Boston's first large-size model and was very much in demand. After some persuasion, she agreed to move to New York, where her friend had opened an agency for large or plus size women. Mary tells her story: "I was making a lot of money modeling in Boston, but I had no right to think I could come back to New York and succeed in the business. I knew nothing about the modeling industry. It was a case of ignorance is bliss. If I had known what I should have known, but I didn't, I would have been hysterical. I learned just in time. I became a partner and when my friend decided to sell, I bought her out." Mary has since written a book on the subject of plus-size models.

Today, top agencies in fashion cities around the world have divisions for models who are size 10 and over. As staggering as it may seem, a size 10 is actually considered a Plus size. Department stores such as Neiman Marcus, Nordstroms and Macy's are now meeting the demand for larger sizes. Georgio

Armani has a Plus line in Europe and American designers have followed suit.

Gary Dakin, a New York agent for Plus-size models told me: "Eighty-five percent of the women in this country are over a size 10. It is inconceivable to have size 4's, 6's and 8's representing the fashion industry." One frustrating aspect of the business for Gary is that the pay is not as good as for 'straight' models –the term used in the industry for the under size ten market. He vows to work on that. He is particularly excited about the teenage models who fall into the Plus category. "They are still working on the acceptance of their size. They look at Vogue and Elle and still see that image. But with the arrival of new magazines such as Mode and with good old standbys such as Big Beautiful Women (BBW), they are starting to say: 'Wow! We're beautiful too. And that is because of, not in spite of, our size.'"

Michele Weston is the fashion and style director of Mode, a fashion and beauty magazine for the Plus size woman. Mode was so successful when it hit the newsstands that production went from four magazines in the first year to ten in the second. I asked Michele how a prospective model should approach a career. She said: "She should go the same route as any other model. Start with local agencies and then branch out to New York, L.A. and other major cities. She has to be prepared for rejection and perseverance is the key. Remember that not everyone is supposed to be a model. There are 8 billion people in the world and only 8 of them are super models."

Beautiful African American model Peggy Dillard was a high fashion international model for ten years. I interviewed Peggy after a flight from London where she had been booked for a major campaign – as a size 10-12 model. She told me: "I had to accept the fact that I was no longer a size 6-8. It meant putting my ego on the shelf and being realistic. Here I was in my late twenties fretting over a little extra weight. Now I don't have the same anxieties. I don't have to ask myself, 'Will the clothes fit? Are the sleeves going to be too short?' What really bothered me during my years as a high fashion model was the number of models depending on drugs to control their weight and the number of models with bulimia. I saw this on a daily basis. I was working with models I had admired in magazines when I was in high school whose motivation for staying thin were drugs and starving themselves. I had to pull away for a year and take that time for reflection. I had worked for all of the top designers, some of whom thought that breasts were unflattering. I was cultivating a sense of schizophrenia. I was living someone else's fantasies. I was ready to live in my own body and to be comfortable with myself. Now I love myself as I am."

Summing up, Plus-size models are size 10, 12, 14, 16 and 18. There are a small number who are size 20 and 24. Height requirement is 5'8"-6'0", with weight in proportion to height. There are large-size markets in the major cities. If you don't have an agency that represents large sizes in your area and you fit this category, it is worthwhile asking the fashion coordinators of local department stores to consider you for future shows. We are seeing more and more Plus-size models in fashion shows. They do a super job and are well received by the audiences.

Petites

The results of the New York fashion market study that produced the startling revelations about the large-size woman did the same for the petite woman. It showed that the average American woman is a little shorter than 5'4" (5'3. 8" to be exact—only one in ten women is 5'10" or over). This meant that a market for petite sizes could be as great as 50 percent of American women.

In spite of these statistics, the job market for the petite model is practically non-existent. Hopes for the future are dim. One agent told me: "It is totally out of the question that a girl who is 5'3" or 5'4" will become a superstar model in New York. As long as big catalog companies can write 'also available in petite' across the bottom of a picture, they will not use petite models. There has to be a reeducation of the petite woman. She must write to the department stores and ask to see petite mannequins modeling clothing. She must write to the catalog companies and ask them to use petite models. She must insist that she be represented as she is—a petite woman. This is what women with full figures did. It became almost a political cause. Now it is a booming industry."

Mary Theresa Zazzera worked in the specialty division of the Ford agency for twelve years. As a consultant to the industry she told me: "This is the most difficult area to address in the entire modeling industry. Runway work is limited to department stores but petites can do print work and they can work in the fit and showroom markets. Book covers are another aspect—many of the girls who work with Fabio are quite diminutive. Also, many petites wear a size six shoe, which is the sample size for shoe photography. A shorter girl can make it in this industry, if she is prepared to spread herself more thinly than other models. As far as a major career? The Kate Mosses are the exception, not the rule!"

In New York, I spoke with Mary Catherine McCarthy, who was

extremely knowledgeable about this specialty, having worked for an agency for petite models. She said: "Photographers often prefer petite models because they have better proportions. Height is only an issue on a runway or in a live performance. Television provides a definite career path for a petite model. Lipstick does not need height. But a petite model must have a beautiful face and a very good figure. Acting ability is a great asset because so much of the work is in television."

David Vando, the owner of Model's Mart in New York is always being asked the question, "I'm a petite, what do I do?" His answer is: "You are not a 'petite' you are a performer, an artist. Learn to sing and dance. Take acting lessons. Learn to be a spokeswoman. There are so many things you can do in this industry, in the Arts."

I discussed the possibilities for petite models in England with Zorina Fleming. She said: "We are seeing opportunities for the slightly shorter model in London. But she must have an incredible face to compensate for the height and a very strong agency behind her."

We discussed the meteoric rise of 5'7" superstar Kate Moss. Kate was 5'6" and fourteen when she was discovered by Sarah Doukas of London's Storm Agency, in a standby lane at J.F.K. Airport. Zorina said: "I'm glad Kate broke the height barrier. But she has an amazing face and is so versatile. She is also represented by a fantastic agency. If Sarah Doukas sends a petite to Vogue, they will agree to look at her because of who Sarah is. If a smaller agency did this, they would say 'Forget it!' Perhaps if Kate had been with a smaller agent they would have said the same to her."

When a client requests a petite model for a job, only a petite model should show up. I am 5'9" and I remember going on a television commercial casting for an alleged luxury yacht. There were several 5'9" blondes at the casting. The interviews became shorter and the casting director more irritable as time wore on. By the time my turn came he was enraged! I learned later that he had specifically asked for petite models. Apparently the "luxury" yacht was on the small side and would have looked like a toy with a five-foot-niner towering on deck!

Parts

There are lucrative specialties for men and women where height, weight and age are not criteria. Models with perfect hands, feet, legs (sorry, chaps, not you!), teeth, eyes and lips have very bankable assets and the sum of the parts makes their agents financially thrilled.

Hand modeling, for example, is versatile and lucrative. An experienced hand model in New York can earn from $75 to $250 an hour for print work. Daily television rates range from $325 to $650. Make no mistake, hand modeling can be as grueling as any other type of modeling. Clients are very specific about the hands that will show their products. A small hand can make a product look bigger and vice versa. Hand models must constantly care for their hands and nails (washing floors and scraping paint is out—oh well, sacrifices have to be made!).

Fit Modeling

Fit models are a very important part of the fashion industry. Men, women and children work directly with designers, pattern makers, manufacturers and buyers. Their job is to tell the designer how an outfit feels when it is worn and show how it will look in real life.

The fit model category, which embraces straight, large and petite, is very much in demand.

The Sports Model

Michael Lyons owns THE LYONS GROUP, the largest sports agency in the country. Although it represents all areas of commercial and catalog print for men, women and children, it specializes in the athlete model. Michael told me: "We represent 37 Olympic athletes, professional athletes and over 120 athletic skills.

Sports advertising has become big in the last few years. Roller blading, snow boarding, soccer, boxing—fitness is in! People like active people. I provide the talent to meet that need."

Older Models

We only have to look at such fabulous models as Lauren Hutton, Christie Brinkley, Cheryl Tiegs and the incredible Carmen, to know that there is an immensely lucrative career for the older model. It is hard to believe that "older" means twenty-five and over.

In Florida there are tremendous opportunities for work in print and film. This has opened up new careers for retirees. However, there is always the problem that these days men and women look much younger than their years. The Disney Corporation has a very definite picture of the ideal grandma or grandpa—white-haired, plump and slightly squinty. Agents find that the talent they send in the required age bracket is often rejected by casting directors for looking too young. The 40+ Model and Talent Agency in Miami represents over 300 men and women, aged 40 and over. Spokeswoman Judi Williams told me: "This is an excellent second career for people from all walks of life."

Physically Handicapped

I have kept track of this category over the years and unfortunately the very few agencies with this focus have not done well.

There is work, however, in film, television and television commercials. In New York, McDonald Richards, Inc. has a division for the physically handicapped.

Chapter
11

Advice from Female Models

The models with whom I spoke, from beginners to superstars, had different stories to tell about how they got started in the business and how it treated them. A consistent thread of information came through in every interview. To succeed as a model you must be professional, persistent, resilient, pleasant and strong enough to stand up for what you believe. I was most impressed with the women I interviewed and found they were very willing to share their experience and knowledge with newcomers. Here are some of their stories.

Carol Alt

Cover model Carol Alt is a superstar with the famous Elite agency in New York. She is an outstanding role model for young girls. Carol is charming, warm, completely unassuming and very professional. It is obvious that she enjoys her work. Carol's rise to fame is virtually an overnight success story. Some years ago, on the first day at her agency, she was told she had to lose 12 pounds. She weighed 145 pounds (she is now 30 pounds slimmer) and was "just a shade under 5'10"." On her first go-see that same day, the lady who interviewed her told her, in Carol's words: "Everything was wrong with me, from my head to my feet!" A photographer and a makeup artist who were at the studio, however, did not agree and insisted she stay while they worked with her. The happy and phenomenal ending to the story is that not only did she get the job, but the shoot also resulted in 92 tear sheets, her first trip to Europe and the cover of Italian Bazaar!

Carol has learned much from her experience as a model and world traveler. I was present when she generously shared this knowledge with over seven hundred prospective models and parents at a modeling convention. Her mother, Mrs. Muriel Alt, who also modeled at one time, shared the stage with her daughter and passed on invaluable tips to mothers. Carol told her enthusiastic audience, "Don't ever compromise. If you have a gut feeling that something isn't right, don't do it! Don't do something that will come back to haunt you. Don't have a picture taken that you wouldn't want to show to your mom and dad or, eventually, your own children."

When a girl in the audience asked her if she had ever been discouraged to the point of giving up, Carol looked at her mother and replied: "Ask my mom how many nights I cried!" Another girl asked her how she felt about her success and her beauty. Carol answered: "I never really thought about being successful. I know that one day I felt I must be doing something right when someone asked me for my opinion about something on the set.... And I certainly never thought I was beautiful." Carol constantly stresses the need for professionalism. She considers it the most important characteristic for a model.

She attributes much of her success to family support. She told the girls at the convention: "Go to your mother and cry if you need to. Get it all out. You will feel a heck of a lot better. I was fortunate to have strong support from my family."

Mrs. Alt has this advice for mothers: "Have confidence in your judgment. Believe that the way you raised your children will pay off. Your standards will be theirs. Believe that!" I asked Mrs. Alt what her feelings were when Carol started her professional career. She told me: "I was too busy raising four children to pipe dream. I was just afraid that Carol might nose-dive. I didn't want her to be hurt. Now it is so wonderful to see her channeling her energies into something she enjoys. She works hard, but she loves what she is doing."

Carol had constant support from her sister Christine, a striking blonde with incredible blue eyes. The Alts are a wonderful family whose strong support has been a major factor in Carol's million-dollar success story.

Sandi Bass

Sandi Bass who lives in Los Angeles is an international scout for Agence Presse in Tokyo. I cannot think of anyone more suited to this role. She worked for the top designers in the world for over ten years, lived in Paris and Tokyo and she and her stockbroker husband know the joys and anxieties of having a teenage daughter—an Elite model—who plans to juggle that career with college. Sandi's story is amazing. Against great odds, success came to her in the person of legendary French designer Givenchy. When she was "this scrawny teenager" he came to Los Angeles looking for models to show his beautiful clothes. He was looking for thin models, but Sandi's agent refused to send her to the interview claiming that she was too thin. Givenchy, however, did not pick any of the models they sent and they finally agreed to send her to meet him. Givenchy booked her to go to Paris for six months. She stayed for ten years! "I worked for Givency as well as Valentino, Yves St. Laurent and all the other top designers. I also modeled in Japan twice a year. When I went to Europe I felt I had finally found a home. I felt somebody liked me. In Los Angeles there just wasn't a market for me—I was too thin and I was African American."

I asked Sandi for advice for young African American models. She said: "It is very difficult for us, but it is getting better. I had a great career, but I had to go to Europe to do it. I would say to my black sisters, if you really want a modeling career, go for it! But don't just look at modeling. Look at acting also. We have to try a little bit harder. We have to offer a little bit more. Go to school. Get an education. Have something to fall back on. I certainly don't want my daughter to put all her eggs in one basket. Don't be afraid to hold on to your dreams. And they will come."

Her advice to parents of all fledgling models is: "Make sure that this is what your son or daughter wants to do and that it isn't something that you want for them. Make sure you have a reputable agent and allow that agent to guide the career. Allow your child to grow. Don't push them. Some mothers want to rush their daughters thinking only of dollars, dollars, dollars. These years are so precious; don't rob them of their childhood. The modeling industry is a serious business. There is great money to be made. But the child must want to do it and the timing must be right."

Ronnie Carol

An exquisite New York beauty who now lives with her family in Los Angeles, Ronnie is a perfect example that success does not have to spoil the person. Her career began the day she popped into the Ford agency on her way home from high school in New York to see what her chances were of becoming a model. She was accepted immediately. Ronnie told me: "I can remember being so stunned. I ran home to tell my mom and she couldn't believe it either."

Ronnie stayed with the Ford agency for twelve years and traveled all over the world on assignments. "I learned so much from Eileen Ford," she told me. "Being in Europe as a Ford model meant I was treated like royalty. I was invited to parties on fabulous yachts and in beautiful homes, but there was always a group of about fifty girls invited. There were no problems. The people who gave the parties were agency contacts and friends of Eileen. They never stepped out of line. They knew that if they did, Eileen would be on their case immediately."

During those years Ronnie lived in New York and went abroad on direct bookings only. Her looks, beauty and natural ability to model made her an instant success. She did not have to spend time getting tear sheets in Europe as most models do today.

Ronnie has also had experience in the executive side of the business. She was president of Elite Model Management in Los Angeles for two and a half years and knows the profession from all angles. She is a good example that there is a life in the business after the fashion runways of the world.

Peggy Dillard

Despite the fact that lovely African American model Peggy Dillard was told by every major model agent in New York to give up the idea of modeling, she enjoyed ten years as a much sought after international couture model. In the beginning she didn't even have a portfolio. "Vogue magazine and all the other editorial clients first saw me on the runway. Peggy told me how it all happened. "I started as a showroom model, which is not considered very glamorous, for Ralph Lauren. Then Ralph used me for his Press campaigns. As he saw that I knew what I was doing, he put me in his shows and I did his editorial work. I think that part of my success was due to the fact that I wasn't a conformist. Everyone told me I should straighten my hair and that I should be super thin. The fact that I didn't straighten my hair and I wasn't super thin, wasn't an obstacle for me. It made me stand apart. I was unique."

Peggy's advice for African Americans who want to be models is: "You don't have to be a superstar to be successful. There are many black women who have been successful in this industry, whether it is on the runway or in catalog, who are not household names. They live somewhat more normal lives. Look at your individual attributes and realize how to market them. Learn everything you can about the business. Do your homework. Approach this business as you would a college project. Find out what photographers are looking for. Go to see the agents and listen to their perspective. Don't be discouraged."

Peggy is now working as a size 10-12 model which is considered a Plus size. She has definite opinions on models who starve themselves to a size 6-8 (see the section on Plus size models). "I want to bring a level of integrity, a touch of class, to my work no matter what size I am wearing."

Gloria Dare

Another extremely successful model who is always willing to share the secrets of her success is Gloria Dare. She has a wealth of knowledge and experience from which to draw, having worked as a fashion model in Rome, Paris, Milan, Zurich and Hong Kong. Her national advertisement clients include: Revlon, Maybelline, Dupont, J.C. Penney, Oscar de la Renta, Revillon Furs, Charles of the Ritz and Lily of France.

Gloria was introduced to modeling when she was fifteen years old. "My mother enrolled me in a modeling course to get me out of the trees—I was such a tomboy," she says. Originally she was with the Wilhelmina Model Agency in New York and her first four years were spent traveling to and from Europe, where she did the Collections. She worked constantly. During the next four years she did a lot of commercial work, which she enjoyed immensely. She explained, "I feel more comfortable doing commercial work, I don't have to worry about tear sheets and it is much more lucrative."

I have watched Gloria teach runway seminars showing girls how to walk and turn. She has endless patience and it pays off. She makes the girls come alive and move beautifully, making the clothes they are wearing take on new meaning. The thrust of her basic teaching is attitude and energy. She told me: "I can teach the basic turns and walk and show the students hand and shoulder movements, but I can't program them on how to act on a runway. A model has to have imagination and be able to change her mood to suit the outfit. I show her all of the options of movement. A runway model must always be aware that she is selling clothes. It is her job to make the audience go out and buy the outfits she is showing and make fashion editors want to feature them in their magazines. Their attitude and the energy they project are all-important. The same goes for guys. The secret is to make it fun. Don't try to model. Just model."

Gloria has this to say to young people who plan to pursue a modeling career: "You will learn so much traveling around the world. It is an education in itself. But formal education is very important. If you are fifteen, finish school. You won't always have your looks, but what you have in your mind you will have forever. From a moral standpoint, if you find yourself in a situation that is not right for you, get out of it. Be strong and do what your conscience tells you is right, no matter what anybody else says or does."

Gloria, who grew up in Charlotte, North Carolina, adds, "Not every city is as clean and friendly as Charlotte and Europe doesn't always have the comforts of home. Modeling is a tough life, but I am a country girl and I believe hard work never hurt anyone.

Gloria is a freelance model with a degree in psychology. She also works as a volunteer with terminally ill children.

Shailah Edmonds

It is an absolute joy to watch Shailah on a runway, whether on her video, teaching a workshop, or in a fashion show. It is an even greater pleasure to interview her. She not only has intelligence and beauty but also a spiritual grace, which illuminates her. She is always smiling and is the very best at what she does. Shailah is a top international model. She was kind enough to write the foreword to this book. Shailah has worked for the top agents in this country and is now a freelance model in demand all over the world. She has this advice: "Stay focused. Stay humble. Don't be intimidated by other models. There will always be somebody who is better than, or not as good, as you. Show compassion for everyone—we are all in this for the same reason. Above all, from the moment you step through the door as a model, be professional. This professionalism never stops. If you are really serious about being a fashion model, practice your walk and runway technique for two or three hours a day. Know the latest makeup and fashion trends. Bring your own makeup, shoes (make sure you can walk on high, spiky heels if that is what is called for) and accessories. Take advantage of the videos that are available."

Shailah has this specific advice for her sister African American models: "The market is smaller and there are a lot of us out there. Any good agency in their representation includes African American or ethnic or minority models. If the model fits the criteria there is a market."

I have seen Shailah at work as a runway model, teaching seminars and in her invaluable instructional video. She can be contacted through Models Mart, New York. Tel. (212) 944-0638.

Tracy Matheson

Tracy was seventeen when she went to Europe to model. She had been accepted at university and deferred her entrance for a year. Teachers told her to forget the modeling and go straight to school. Model agents said college could wait, the time to model was now. Tracy struggled with the dilemma, made a decision, packed her bags and left for Europe.

She was fortunate to have modeled for a number of years. Tracy had an impressive portfolio, tear sheets and several commercials—three of them national—to her credit. She had earned her fare to Europe and money to support herself. This experience, plus the fact that she is 5'10" tall, weighs 128 pounds and has blond hair and blue eyes, meant that she had distinct advantages. However, if she was to succeed in this highly competitive market, she had to make the necessary leap from regional to international modeling and put together a European composite and strong portfolio.

It was difficult at first. Tracy found that understanding different customs, struggling with foreign languages and leading the life of a fledgling model on the international scene was a challenge. There were a few tearful transatlantic phone calls in the first month, but these always ended in adamant refusals to return to the security of home and family. Her resilience, determination and immeasurable joie-de-vivre paid off. She did designer shows, posters, catalog work, television commercials and acquired a new composite, tear sheets—and her first cover. Says Tracy, "I was lucky. So often I was in the right place at the right time. I remember one day flying into Germany from a little island off the coast of Denmark where I had been on a fashion assignment. I went straight from the airport to my agency. I had no makeup on and I was wearing a jogging suit. There was an important Swiss client in the next room whom I was supposed to see. I told my booker I had to wash my hair and change clothes before I met the client. To my horror the lady, who represented a very big company and an important account for my agency, walked through the door. She stood and looked at me and said, 'I want this girl just as she is, completely natural.' I was floored! On another occasion I had just arrived in Milan and the Why Not Agency sent me on a go-see for a magazine cover. My agent told me that although my portfolio was not yet strong enough for Milan, the interview and exposure would be good experience. I went—and I got the cover assignment. You just never know what is going to happen—or when."

Tracy's career, however, didn't move into top gear until she met Sonja (Soni) and Ralf Eckvall, who own Model Team—one of the world's top agencies—in Hamburg, Germany. There was instant mutual admiration and respect. Soni knew that Tracy's classic look was the main ingredient for her success. She encouraged her to work only with this look and not change hair or makeup to conform to fashion fads or to please the whims of photographers—a mistake many young models make. Soni has an almost Pygmalion touch in shaping and molding her models. Etiquette, exquisite manners, culture and diplomacy are considered as important to a model's career as are knowing how to walk, turn and move in front of a camera. She encourages her models to become part of European life, to learn the languages, meet people and understand the different cultures. The results are remarkable. By the end of the year Tracy had not only modeled in Milan, Paris, Zurich, Munich, Hamburg and Scandinavia, but she could speak German, French and Italian with reasonable fluency and had made friends all over Europe. Her stay had included a couple of memorable vacations—a skiing holiday in the Swiss Alps and a trip to the Greek Islands.

Tracy returned to the States and was represented by the Nina Blanchard Model Agency in Los Angeles while she attended UCLA. She wanted to go to medical school and hoped that she could do this and model as well. Once in medical school she realized this could not be. She had to make a decision—modeling or medicine. She is now a doctor doing post graduate work in radiology. "Modeling taught me discipline and perseverance which I found invaluable in medical school. The traveling I did always gives me something to talk about—besides medicine!"

Her advice to new models: "Believe in yourself one hundred percent. Self-assurance is so important. Be friendly and adaptable—clients and photographers don't want prima donnas, they want models who are down-to-earth and easy to work with. And be patient. At first, you will think you are never going to make it. Then your career takes off. You are booked, rebooked and prebooked. Suddenly there are new girls sitting around asking the questions you asked. Now it is your turn to console, encourage and advise. You know you are on your way. It is a great feeling!"

As parents, my husband and I experienced a great thrill when we arrived in Europe and saw Tracy smiling at us from billboards and magazines!

Sara Olson

When Sara first arrived in New York as a teenager she found it so overwhelming that she returned to her home in Cedar Rapids, Iowa, for six months before tackling it again. Her career was launched on an international level, though, with the assistance of her mother agent, Mary Brown. When I met Sara she was represented by IMG in New York and top agencies in Dallas, Chicago and Miami. Sara told me: "Just because a girl is blessed with a beautiful body and face doesn't mean she can sit at home and eat. She has to watch her weight, exercise and go on go-sees. A lot of girls won't go on go-sees because they are too tired. This is hard work. It's not about a limo picking you up at the door or wearing expensive clothes."

I asked her for specific advice for fledgling models. She said: "Be confident! Be outgoing! Be yourself! But if you are too quiet, agents will think you are standoffish. Realize that other people feel just like you. Always be loyal to your mother agent. Mine changed my life. I wouldn't be where I am now without her."

Beverly Peele

When she was thirteen, Beverly was spotted by a Los Angeles agent at an International Model and Talent Association convention. Within months, Beverly was modeling in New York and Milan and appeared on the cover of Mademoiselle magazine. At the time, I asked Beverly about her new career and how her schoolmates treated her. She said: "It was overwhelming to arrive in Milan. But it was neat. I was really excited to be out of America for the first time. My schoolmates asked me how I got started and what it is like to be a model. I tell them a little about it—I don't want to sound as if I'm bragging—and then I slowly change the subject."

After high school Beverly was established as an international model. She is African American and 5'11" tall. She now has a daughter Cairo. Beverly was back on a fashion shoot three weeks after her daughter's birth. She took baby Cairo to Rome, Milan and Paris for the shows. They were photographed together for a fashion spread in Allure magazine.

Beverly had the support of loving parents. Her mother, Dr. Lucia Peele is an assistant high school principal and her father John is a patent lawyer.

Gabrielle Reece

Gabrielle "Gabby" Reece is 6'3" and possesses a look that conveys both athleticism and beauty. At nineteen, Gabby was an international cover model and a star athlete—the pride of Florida State University's volleyball team. In her sophomore year, Elle magazine named her "one of the five most beautiful women in the world."

Gabby was discovered by Coral Weigel, an international talent scout.

Coral met Gabby when she was in high school and knew then that she had the potential to be a top model. Coral told me: "I knew that no agent would look at a girl who was six three at that time. Even six feet was too tall for New York. And Gabby had to finish school. But I knew that Gabby was special. I knew she was star material."

As high school ended, athletic scholarships came in and Gabby accepted one for FSU. During a summer vacation Coral decided it was time for Gabby to go to New York. One agent told me: "When I saw Gabby and realized she was six three I told her she would either really make it in the business, or she would do nothing at all. She told me, 'Fine. That's what I expected. If it really happens, I'll be very happy and if it doesn't, I'll continue to play volleyball.' She had a great attitude." The agency received major bookings for her for the Fall but had to turn them down because Gabby had made a commitment to her volleyball coach and team. Gabby continued to juggle schoolwork and volleyball games to find time for modeling assignments. She spent her final spring break from college in Paris modeling for the famous designer Valentino.

Gabby has been a correspondent for MTV Sports and a contributing editor for Elle magazine. Now a professional athlete, she was a Nike spokesperson for woman's athletics and captained the Nike team in the Women's Beach Volleyball League. She now plays two-person pro beach volleyball. During the season she spends three hours in the gym in the morning and the rest of the day playing volleyball. She is internationally recognized as a top fashion model— Gabby has been on the cover of many magazines including Shape, Elle, Fitness, Self, Men's Fitness, Bazaar, Vogue and Women Sports & Fitness, for which she is a columnist. She is a spokesperson for several companies. She co-authored, with Karen Karbo, a book entitled, *Big Girl in the Middle*, about her life as a professional athlete. The television program Lifetime for Women profiled Gabby on its biography series.

Fame has not affected her outlook on life. Gabby took time out of a hectic schedule for an interview. She gave me this advice for new models: "Realize what is important to you in your life. Don't make modeling the number-one thing. Keep your career in perspective. Learn how to invest money and get everything that is good out of modeling."

What a career! What a role model! Gabby is now married to world famous surfer Laird Hamilton.

Barbara Smith

African American model Barbara Smith had a successful international career as a Wilhelmina model. She appeared on the covers of Essense, Ebony and Mademoiselle. Her dream was to save enough money to open a restaurant, which she did. B. SMITH'S, her restaurant at the corner of 8th Avenue and 47th Street is enormously popular with the theatre crowd. Barbara has another equally popular restaurant in Union Square, Washington, D.C. Still busy doing national television commercials, Barbara has a very successful television show, B. Smith's Style, which is produced by her husband, Dan Gasby. She has also written a cookbook entitled Entertaining and Cooking for Friends.

Top model, TV star, author and restaurateur! Barbara is proof that if you hold on to your dreams they can come true. She is a great role model!

Sarah Webb

Although beautiful, Ford model Sarah Webb's first year in Paris was slow and blotted with rejection. She then appeared in every major fashion magazine. To girls who are planning to become models who may even at this moment be sitting in Paris, Milan, or London wondering if they are ever going to make it, Sarah had this to say: "Be patient and stay where you are. Don't waste money on airfare home and back again. It takes a long time to get established, but you will make it eventually. Don't make the mistake of comparing yourself with other girls. That can destroy you. I know it hurts when a friend gets a job you tried out for. But your turn will come. Remember, the client's decision had nothing to do with you as a person. Your look was just not right at that time."

Sarah grew up in Memphis, Tennessee, where she modeled during high school. A hometown photographer sent her pictures to the Ford agency in New York and Sarah received a call from Eileen Ford asking her to go to New York. Sarah told me: "Eileen said she wanted to see if I was really the girl in the photographs." Sarah went to New York with her parents, met Eileen Ford and was accepted. Before modeling professionally, however, she went to a university and studied French history for eighteen months. But the urge to model became very strong and she decided to devote all of her energy to a modeling career. She was sent by Ford Models to the Karin Model Agency in Paris. The first six months were slow, with a lot of rejection, but by the end of the year Sarah had a book full of tear sheets and was ready to work in New York.

Her advice to young girls starting a career in modeling: "Always stand by your morals and your boundaries. A girl who thinks she is going to make it in this business by sleeping around will be all washed up in six months. Sometimes a photographer will try to take advantage of her because he figures a new girl is naïve and gullible. This is when she must make a stand and tell him she will leave unless she is treated with respect. Be very straightforward and businesslike. Once this is established there will be no more problems. They get the message very quickly. Always be true to yourself. This is a cruel profession and people will hurt you. But you will build character and become strong."

Chapter
12

Advice from Male Models

The guys in the business are a superstratum of dedication, determination, intelligence and masculinity. They are incredibly good looking. The dedication of female models is taken for granted. But men take the business just as seriously. They diet and work out daily. They read the Wall Street Journal, study the stock market and talk investments. They model to make money—a lot of money—and see the world. This was one of the surprises I experienced while researching this book. I had no idea that modeling for men was such a respected and lucrative profession. The good news is that a man's career lasts much longer than a woman's; the bad news is his earning power is much less. This is not likely to change.

One New York booker in the male division of an agency told me: "It has become much more acceptable for a man to become a model. In Italy there are a lot fashion magazines for men who study them and gear their style to that trend. Here, there are fewer magazines, but men are starting to read about fashion and to take a greater interest in what they wear. It has become acceptable for men to be interested in fashion."

Some men got into the profession by accident and treated it as a bit of a joke at first. But when money started pouring in and New York, Paris and Milan became home they saw the potential for a financially rewarding career and world travel. They realized this is a serious business and that self-discipline and total dedication are essential if they are to succeed—even guys get bags under the eyes after too many late nights!

I listened to their stories with increasing amazement. Some became instant successes, while others had to suffer initial months of rejection.

Dodge Billingsley

Dodge shook his head in disbelief when he talked about his success story. He was helping on the staff at a modeling convention in Florida when he was spotted by an agent from Spain. At the time he didn't have pictures, portfolio, or passport. The passport obtained, he stepped off the plane in Madrid a week later and went to work. There were few idle moments after that.

Dodge was born in Los Angeles, the oldest of eight children. His first brush with modeling came when he took part in a couple of fashion shows organized by the student government at Brigham Young University, where he was studying political science and international relations. He remembered enjoying the experience but thought nothing more about it. He spent two years on a mission for the Mormon Church, after which he returned to his home in Phoenix. His blond hair and striking, rugged looks caught the attention of a local agency. Through them he worked at the modeling convention in Miami which is where he was scouted by the agent from Madrid. The rest is a success story.

When Dodge arrived in Madrid he went straight to his agency, was given his first casting, got the job and left that night for a three-day shoot in the Mediterranean. He didn't even have time to unpack. His first shoot produced a picture good enough for the front of his composite and tear sheets that were sent to the famous Riccardo Gay Agency in Milan. It happened again. This time Dodge was prebooked for a three-day shoot. He arrived in Milan and didn't meet his agent until the third day of the assignment.

I asked Dodge what advice and warnings he would pass on to boys and girls going into the modeling profession. He said: "A New York agent told me that a lot of models go to Europe to play. When I got there I saw that was true. Believe me, that just doesn't work. It is a serious business. If I didn't get to bed at 10:00 or 11:00 p.m., I couldn't be serious about working the next morning. You can't treat your time in Europe as if it were a vacation."

Scott Goodrich

Much can be learned from blond, ruggedly handsome Scott Goodrich. Scott was born in Atlanta, Georgia. He grew up in military surroundings. After high school Scott went to the College of William and Mary on a full athletic scholarship and played football for four years. He graduated with a degree in

Psychology. Six months later he was modeling in Europe.

It all began in his senior year when he went to a modeling competition to provide moral support for his sister, who was a competitor. A scout from a New York model agency spotted him and advised him to lose weight and start modeling. Scott was 6'2" and 235 pounds at the time—great statistics for a football player but not a model. With his football days almost over, he embarked on a physical fitness campaign. He ran five miles a day and cut his calories to 1,000 a day. He lost 60 pounds, thought more about what the scout said and headed for Paris. He had $400, no portfolio and no pictures. Scott told me: "I starved for about six months and could barely make ends meet." But the starving and hard work paid off. Scott landed a major designer clothing campaign and never looked back. With his pictures in GQ, Vogue, Harper's Bazaar and other major magazines, he was in demand all over the world.

Scott told me about his weight loss and how his background and upbringing had helped him achieve a successful career. "First of all I told myself that if I couldn't control my own weight, I could not hope to control anything else in my life. I lost my excess pounds with a strict diet and a hell of a lot of exercise and discipline. When I was a kid my family traveled a lot in the military. I went to ten schools in twelve years! This made me develop great adjustment skills. Playing football for ten years made me very competitive. Discipline, adaptability and competitive spirit are excellent qualities for a model. I model for money and that's it. I save 75 percent of what I make and plan to invest every cent. I have learned far more from my travel experiences than any university textbook could teach me. I don't sell books, vacuum cleaners, or refrigerators. I sell me—and that's one hell of a management job."

Patrick Johnson

Patrick has the classic, all-American look. His career has spanned twenty years and is still going strong. He is in demand as a runway, print and catalog model, an actor and drama coach. His charisma and special gift of imparting knowledge have made the workshops and acting classes he teaches in New York very successful.

Patrick told me that his career has not always been on the crest of a wave. There have been ups and downs and at times He has been very discouraged. In the beginning he was at the point of giving up entirely. Then his career suddenly took off. "I was an engineering major at Arizona State and had no desire to be a model. However, when an opportunity presented itself I thought I would give it a try. I was miserable. For the first three months in New York I had my bags packed every day ready to leave. My brother thought it was the opportunity of a lifetime and encouraged me to stay. He said that if I would give it six months he would do everything to get me back into school if things didn't work out. I felt better. I had a goal—a plan. This gave me a new state of mind. Almost immediately things started to fall into place. I got a spread in GQ and this led to a campaign in Italy. My career snowballed. And I'm still here, seventeen years later."

At one point, however, Patrick tried to switch careers. "At the time I was tired of rejection. I was burned out and thought 'I can't do this anymore.' I went to school, got my real estate license and a company to represent me. One day I sat in the office and looked at all the people around me and I said to myself, 'I know that I can do what they do, but they can't do what I do. Who's kidding whom? I changed course again. From that moment my career was on an upward swing in acting, modeling and television. It is all in your frame of mind. You have got to believe in yourself and be happy in what you are doing. So much of you is in your face, in your attitude, in the way you speak, in the way you communicate with people. If you are unhappy and lacking self-confidence, it is difficult to walk in and get a director to believe in you and want to hire you for a commercial"

Discussing the misconceptions aspiring male and female models have, Patrick said: "They see boys and girls who are making money and who seem to be having a great time. They don't see the long working days, the lonely weeks spent in Europe and the disillusionment when people you trust mislead you. But if they know about this side and they have the interest and the talent, they can be successful. It is an ideal job for a young guy who doesn't really know what he wants to do with his life. He can travel, make money and then after five years move on. He should see this job as a stepping stone to another career.

"I can say that this is a great business because I am working. There were times when I would not have encouraged anyone to come into it. There are no guarantees. Getting an agent doesn't mean you are going to work. One job doesn't necessarily mean there will be another. It is a very insecure business because you don't know what is going to happen tomorrow. Everyone wants to feel secure and know that tomorrow they will have enough money. In this business you have to live for the moment. If this career is your dream—pursue it. But be informed and be professional. Most of all be happy."

Keith Knutsson

An example of someone who has maintained excellent basic values, at nineteen years of age Keith was one of the youngest men to model in Europe and enjoyed phenomenal success. He put his modeling career on hold to go back to continue his college education.

During his high school senior year in Clearwater on Florida's Gulf Coast, he had his first contact with the modeling profession. He was at the boat docks with his girlfriend one day cleaning his boat, when a representative from a large boat and sporting equipment company approached him and asked if he would take part in a publicity campaign. He told Keith that if he showed up the next day, he could ride around in one of the company's boats and earn $65 an hour while they took photographs. Keith was dubious but arrived on time the next day. "My girlfriend and I had a great time driving around in a boat all day. I made a lot of money. I thought it was a joke. I took the money and as far as I was concerned that was the end of it."

His striking looks and great body were not to go unnoticed. While he was earning money during school holidays as a bellboy at a resort hotel in Florida, a model agent saw Keith and advised him to have pictures taken for a composite. His quick reply was: "You wouldn't say that if you saw my driver's license picture." The agent persisted, however and eventually Keith had photographs taken and couldn't believe the results. "I just couldn't believe that was me in the photographs," he said. Once again he forgot about modeling, forgot about the pictures and went to college to study medicine. His father insisted he concentrate on his studies and not work. Keith told me: "I had always had a job during high school to earn money to take my girlfriend out and have a good time. I didn't want to ask my dad for money and he didn't want me to work." He remembered the lucrative day he had spent doing publicity shots in Florida, found the photographs he had had taken and took them to a model agent in South Carolina. The immediate result was two television commercials and print work.

About that time a scout arrived from a New York model agency and saw Keith. She told him he would be leaving for Milan the following week. He replied: "No way! I'm leaving for my chemistry class next week. Sorry!" As summer vacation approached, his local agent sent Keith's pictures to all the top New York agents. Ford, Wilhelmina, Zoli, Legends and several other agents asked to see him. He told me: "I went to New York and saw them all. They seemed interested and they all wanted to send me to Europe. I was very naïve about the business, but I realized I was very lucky to see these people, never mind have each one want to sign me. But everything seemed wishy-washy. Nothing was concrete. I was used to working with my father, a businessman, who liked everything to be cut and dried. I was so overwhelmed and confused I was ready to forget it. However, the Ford agency arranged an appointment with Karin from Karin's Model Agency, a Ford affiliate, in Paris. This time everything was organized and three weeks later I found myself in Paris!" Keith was nineteen when he arrived—one of the youngest male models to work in Europe. He worked constantly in Paris, Milan, Germany and even Japan. "That was amazing because at 6'1½", I was tall for Japan. They cut an awful lot of sleeves out of an awful lot of shirts when I worked."

After two years of traveling the world and making a lot of money, Keith decided he wanted to return to the U.S. and go back to school. "I can remember the day I made that decision I was shooting a commercial in Paris. We had been on the set all day, which was normal. Everything was wild and crazy and I thought, 'I have to get out of this for a while.' I wanted to be able to control my own destiny. I knew that if I went back to school I could do this."

He started his senior year studying business at Emory University in Atlanta, Georgia. He chose Emory because he liked all aspects of the university and knew that he could model in the young, progressive Atlanta market. He especially wanted to "blend into college life and be a normal student." He was obliged to have an answering service so that his Atlanta agent could contact him. This meant that he had to confide to his roommate that he was a model, emphasizing that he wanted this to remain a secret. This was not to be. His father arrived brandishing a copy of Vogue containing pictures of Keith; his roommate talked, and Keith's picture appeared that month in GQ magazine. The news was out. "It was awful. No one would talk to me. The girls stood back and whispered, 'He's the guy in GQ.' Fortunately this didn't last too long and I was able to enjoy a normal life as a student." Keith became president of his pledge class and a member of the swim team. He quickly found that his experiences in Europe and Japan were a great asset in his business courses. "I also really learned the value of money when I was abroad. My classes at Emory were expensive and I couldn't afford to miss one. While my parents paid tuition, I worked to pay for food, clothing, my car, furniture and other expenses."

Keith's excellent advice to young men and women thinking about or starting a modeling career is: "Find out from agents in major markets such as New York, Chicago, or Los Angeles, if you are right for the profession. If you are not, don't waste any more time. Decide on another profession. You never know how long your modeling career will last, so when you make money, invest it. Get advice about investments. Make sure you are financially secure outside of the profession. Exercise to stay in shape. Lead a good life. And don't ever compromise what you believe in. That's very important."

David Martin

David started modeling during his freshman year at he University of Iowa. "One of the sororities was doing a fashion show and they asked me to model in it." David is a drama major whose career spans modeling and acting. Discussing the market for African-American models, he said: "The market is smaller for African-American models—and there are a lot of us who want to be in the business. Things will get better." David draws on twenty years of expertise to pass on this advice: "Go to see all the agents. Really learn the business. When you get a runway show, make sure you know who the stage manager is or who will be giving instruction. Check out the runway and find out where the creases are in it. Always check all of your clothes before the show. Get a manicure and pedicure in advance. Pack your accessories ahead of time. Wear two pairs of socks, dark over light if that is the sequence of the show. Make sure you have an education. If modeling doesn't work out as you had hoped, you will have something else you can do. You can't be a dumb model. You have to be able to read those contracts and understand every detail."

David has modeled in the fashion capitals of Europe, but now prefers to work in this country. "I've loved the places I have seen. But I like being home in the United States."

Kevin Menard

The director of the men's division of a top New York model agency, Kevin Menard is a former model who has a degree in international trade and finance. Kevin told me about his modeling career. "I started in Louisiana with a small agency. Everyone told me I should go to New York, that agents there would send me to Europe. I heard this and saw stars. I was fresh out of college and ready to go. I bought a one-way ticket to New York, walked into an agency but was not prepared for the 'Who sent you?' attitude. I realized that it was not going to be as easy as I had been told. I spent some time testing and then took myself to Italy. It was very hard and I knew I just didn't have the commitment. A booker in Milan took me aside and we had a heart to heart talk. She showed me the file of a guy whose look was very similar to mine who had been modeling for eight years. She said, 'This model has your look and it would take three years of constant testing before we could establish your career. You have to really want to do this.' I thought to myself, 'You know what, I really don't. I want to do something else with my life.' It really takes that commitment. I wanted to travel. Modeling came second. That was my vehicle and it should have been the other way around. I'm so glad I had that conversation with the booker."

Kevin loves the fashion industry and loves sales. That is why today he is one of the best agents for men in the country. "An agent sells talent. I found my niche doing that. If you really love the business, there is always something you can move into. I know models who have become agents, photographers, personal managers, art directors, hair stylists and makeup artists. When I see male models getting frustrated because nothing is happening, I remember Milan and sit down and have a talk with them. I tell them, 'This is the business and this is what it takes. If you want it, get your butt out of town and over to Europe. Leave your girlfriend, leave your car—go! Don't waste time. It won't happen overnight. It will take a long time and a lot of hard work before you see any return financially.' To any kid who thinks of postponing school, or of modeling in lieu of going to school, I would say, 'School comes first. You must have an education.'"

A.J. Vincent

The lesson that can be learned from A.J. Vincent is that a model's enthusiasm and dedication should be placed ahead of financial consideration and the money will automatically take care of itself. A.J. is a successful working model and actor. His personality and attitude are enthusiastic and positive. He loves his chosen career, which is one of the reasons he excels at it. During an interview he explained: "The male market has changed in the last few years. It has grown and is a very well respected place to work. But it is still the same story. If the budget for a job has to be cut, it is the male model who is dropped."

A.J. has this to say to prospective male models: "Go into the business with all the excitement, energy and enthusiasm you can muster. Stay in it because you love it, not just for the glamour and financial reward. Your reward should come from doing good work. On the subject of rejection he says: "Rejection is a strange thing. You can try out for ten jobs and not get one of them. The client will tell you, you are not right—they don't mean you personally. They mean your look is not right to sell their particular product at that time. Then you will try out for a job and you will get it because you are absolutely perfect for that job. And they will tell you that you are absolutely perfect for what they want. It's a great feeling."

Chapter 13

Advice from Other Professionals

I have interviewed a wide variety of key people in the modeling industry worldwide as well as experts in the acting profession. They were very generous with their time, advice and information. They agreed, without exception, that a thorough understanding of what is involved in pursuing a career is essential. They also agreed that this information should only be obtained from legitimate sources. All were concerned with the increasing number of scams and the plight of the victims. Their comments and the answers to many other frequently asked questions follow.

Parents often wonder if they have made the right decision when they allow their child to postpone college to embark on a modeling career. I asked the advice of professionals and feel one fashion coordinator was right on target when she said: "If a girl is bright, she will always be bright, but she won't always have the opportunity to model. If she gets the chance, she should take it." Milan model agent Beatrice Traissac said: "Models are getting younger, especially in America. Even nineteen is too late to start a career." A New York photographer said: "At twenty-five, a doctor is just starting her career, but a model is a has-been."

Model agent Gerard Bisignano said: "Many parents are hesitant to let their child get into this business, but if a child has potential and wants to do it, parents should let them try. Keep the lines of communication open. A girl who has a problem in Europe shouldn't be afraid to call home because her parents might say 'I told you so'. It means supporting your child in a field where the chances of success are certainly not as great as in another industry, but the payoffs are tremendous."

Coral Weigel, an international scout who discovered super model and athlete Gabrielle Reece, had this advice for parents: "Mothers often ask me if I think their daughters can cope with an international modeling career. They worry and ask if their daughters will be chaperoned. I tell them that only they can be the judge of their daughters' capability to deal with the situations and that model agents don't have the time to babysit. I also tell them that if a girl is mature and trustworthy, she will make it."

An agent who spent years scouting for models in the fashion capitals of the world told me, "One of the problems is communication, especially in Italy and France. American girls are very serious about romance. They think that when someone is flirting with them, that person is in love with them. The French and Italian men just enjoy the flirtation. The Milanese playboys just like to be around pretty girls and know where the action is and who is in the modeling business. Girls shouldn't go alone to their apartments or get themselves into a bad situation.

"Another major problem is rejection. Most of the models who are successful are those who don't deal with this business from a personal viewpoint. They treat it like a business and realize that it is all a matter of the right girl, or boy, with the right look, being in the right city at the right time. I believe that this profession is an education in life. The experience can be transferred to any number of professions later on."

Randy Kirby is a multitalented actor, commercial casting director and writer. He has produced over one hundred commercials for radio and television and has won a prestigious Clio award. I asked Randy for a few helpful hints for models who may be sent on television commercial castings. He told me: "The secret is to treat the camera as your best friend. Don't think of it as an object but as someone who likes and trusts you and will, therefore, believe what you have to say about the product you are selling. Once you have the feeling you are talking to a good friend, you will relax and your message will come across with sincerity."

Englishman Larry Conroy has a background in film, theater and radio and has trained corporate and news media personalities. He has also "retrained" some of the world's top models who, as a result of his expertise, combine lucrative television careers with modeling. His workshop, "The

Model Speaks," is sought by those who realize that today, being able to act and speak on camera is a priority. Larry told me: "There is a great market right now for show hosts and field reporters in various cable programs. Models and other people with a good background in fashion are in demand. It doesn't matter how good your voice is, it's how you use it and what you do with it that counts. It's a fact of life—models need to be trained in this area."

Jacques Silberstein has photographed almost every top model in the world. He can make the ingenue look ready for a glossy cover in minutes. It is a privilege to see him create his magic. Jacques took time out of a hectic schedule at his photo-video studio in New York to pass on this advice in his inimitable French accent: "A lot of girls dream of being top models but what they don't realize is that there is hard work and frustration involved. I advise girls planning to work in Europe to check out the people with whom they will work. This is a new world for them and a lot of people want to take advantage of them. Models must be established with a reliable agent and have enough money to return home if life is not what they expected, or if they can't take the pressure."

I asked Jacques what a young girl should do if a photographer should behave unprofessionally. He said: "I have always told any girl who goes to Europe that there is no reason in the world she should do something that she doesn't feel is right. If she does it once, it will never end. The girls who are the happiest in the business are those who are happy with themselves. A girl must stand by her morals."

Tim Tew is a photographer in Orlando, Florida. Tim's business has increased rapidly in the last few years partly because of the quality of his work and partly because of the burgeoning film and television industry in Central Florida. Tim said: "Any girl from any place can be the next super model. New York is always looking. Modeling is acting without words. It used to be considered that if you were a model you couldn't act and if you were an actress you probably didn't have the looks to model. Now we have the actress/model, especially in Central Florida. You have got to know your business and be willing to learn." Tim has great rapport with children and part of his business is devoted to shooting head shots for them. His advice to parents: "Don't let anyone sell you a thousand-dollar portfolio. You only need a couple of snapshots to find out if an agent is interested. Then a good head shot is all you need to get started."

International photographer Mac Hartshorn is always being asked by young models to arrange their portfolios. His advice: "If you ask 50 different people how to put 20 photographs together you will get 50 different opinions. Rely on your agent who knows what the clients want. Basically, if you are a model the first picture should be a head shot geared to fashion and if you are an actor or commercial model, the first picture should be a commercial shot."

Vincent Lappas, an actor, director and coach in Los Angeles, had this to say to young people embarking on an acting career: "You don't earn a part, you win it, by being better than the people you are up against. Talent is a marriage of craft and instinct—if you don't have the craft you won't excel. There are no overnight success stories. You may become famous overnight but it takes years and years of practice."

Determination, hard work and the ability to survive rejection are some of the qualities Adam Hill instills into his students. He is artist-in-residence in the professional theatre department of Wilkes University (which he laughingly explained is, "two hours and four years from Broadway"). Adam had this to say, "Who has the right to tell a 4'10½", balding, fat man, with a terrible New York accent, that he hasn't the remotest chance of becoming an actor. I'm talking of course of Danny De Vito. No one has that right. Success does not depend solely on how you look.

"Everyone has been rejected. All but one of the famous actresses who auditioned for Scarlet O'Hara were rejected. Not everyone is wanted right away. Meryl Streep became a movie star at the age of thirty-six—she didn't just blossom into one. Kevin Costner worked as a janitor in a movie studio. He didn't make it until he was in his thirties. Robert DeNiro wasn't born with a S.A.G. card and neither was Dustin Hoffman. They had to go out and earn it. A lot of doors were opened for Heather Locklear in the beginning because she was so gorgeous. But she cried the blues to me because she felt she wasn't ready. I knew she wasn't. She worked very, very hard for two years and learned how to be a good actress."

Canadian-born, identical twins, Colleen Hoffman and Frannie Andrews were successful runway, print and television commercial models until the end of high school. They worked as a team. They continued to do "twin" commercials but as they were identical they could not compete with each other as models. Frannie went off to university and Colleen opened a modeling school. After college Frannie was successful as an international model while Colleen was successfully immersed in the training and education part of the business. Ill health ended Frannie's career. A damaged immune system caused problems associated with allergies and skin sensitivities. She didn't know it at the time, but one of these problems would open the door to another challenging career. She was unable to use any of the available cosmetic and skin care products. The sisters were motivated to research and finally develop make up and skin care products which Frannie could use.

Colleen founded a company which enabled them to market and share these products with women who had similar skin problems. For Charlotte Whaley, a custom fashion designer, with allergy problems so severe that she has had to be hospitalized from time to time, the new products were literally a life-saver. Charlotte became Colleen's partner. I met the glamorous, talented trio at an I.M.T.A. convention in New York. They were the make-up artists for contestants. Charlotte told me: "There are so many women who cannot use the products in department stores. When models fall into this category it is a serious problem. Colleen and Frannie know what is needed for film and print work and we provide that product."

Frannie said: "I had to give up my modeling career but now I can be involved with our skin care business. It is so fulfilling. Every young model should think of the future and what they can do after modeling, especially if their career is cut short as mine was." Colleen added: "Make-up artistry is a great career. Not everyone is cut out to model. As a school director I feel we must be honest with these young people and direct them to other areas in the industry where they can excel."

Cathrine Granlund always wanted to be a singer but was not allowed as a child to pursue her dreams. She tried real estate and banking but was always drawn to the entertainment industry. "The closest I have come to being a singer was working as a makeup artist on music videos. For me, working with all of those singers was close enough to fulfilling my dream." Cathrine loves her work. Her list of credits on films and television are awesome. She told me: "I can make a difference to the ultimate performance. I am the last person the model or actor sees before going in front of the camera. I apply emotional makeup as well as the other kind. I can boost an actor's morale, or ego, or confidence, with a few words. I have found my fulfillment behind the camera."

Shannon Brown is a model with beautiful, classic features. Although she fits all the criteria for this career her sights are set on an acting career. She already has impressive credits on television. She considers modeling, "my waitress job which supports me while I pursue my acting career." She told me:

"I find acting much more fulfilling. It has more depth. It is so much more than just standing around looking pretty." Her advice to models wanting to make the transition is: "A pretty face might get you through the door but that is it. Take acting lessons. Find a reputable manager. You need to be guided by people who know what they are doing and love what they do." Shannon is also studying singing.

Shannon was originally managed by her mother, Janice (Jan) Brown, who co-owns Talent Management and Entertainment Consultants in Santa Clarita, California, with Debra-Lynn Findon. Jan experienced the anxieties of a mother with a beautiful daughter in show business and those of a manager dedicated to promoting her client. She found that the conflict of her two roles interfered with the warm mother-daughter relationship they both treasured. "I would get on to Shannon about being professional. I expected more of her than any other client. I knew that the business relationship was hurting our friendship. I decided to hand the managerial role over to Debra-Lynn. Once I had done this, everything returned to normal." Jan's advice to young models is: "Be cautious and don't compromise your morals. Be true to yourself. Be careful of the scams that are ready to take your money."

Jan and Debra-Lynn firmly believe that finishing high school should be a top priority. They also believe in developing the careers of new talent slowly. When choosing agents and acting classes, they make sure that the actors they represent talk to several agents and sit in on a number of acting classes, before the final decisions are made. Debra-Lynn told me: "Children need to be children. They can still have a career at eighteen when they have finished school. We like our new talent to start with small parts. We build their careers slowly. We don't put them into a series right away. It is too overwhelming for a child who is not from a big city. They can't handle it. We nurture their careers. Above all, we want these young people to be comfortable and happy with the decisions we all make."

Aaron Marcus is a very good example of the old adage, 'Bloom where you are planted.' Aaron lives in Baltimore, Maryland. He was in his late twenties earning a living as a classical guitarist when, after eight years of absence, he decided to go back to college. His ambition was to be a physical therapist. He needed a job to support himself, a job that was, "really enjoyable, paid a lot per hour and had hours that were flexible." Aaron had always been fascinated with radio and television commercials and magazine advertisements.

He decided to investigate that type of work. "I put myself through two years of college as a part-time actor and commercial model. I loved the work. When it came time to apply for physical therapy school I was having doubts. I wanted to try acting and modeling full-time. I had just become engaged. I knew that my new plans offered no stability, no guaranteed income and crazy hours. More importantly, I didn't know if I would enjoy doing this work on a full-time basis. My fiancée was completely supportive and I plunged ahead. I got more work than I ever imagined and I loved it! Now, this is how I earn my living." Aaron began his career with one small agent in Baltimore –"not the Mecca for the acting world." He now works for sixty-three agents and travels all over the country. He said: "Most people think you have to live in New York, Los Angeles, Chicago or Miami to survive. Some smaller markets have excellent photographers and wonderfully creative art directors. You never know what a small town assignment can lead to. A job in Lancaster, Pennsylvania, can lead to a booking in Alaska."

I asked Aaron to explain his success. He said: "It is not pure coincidence that the people who work the most have the best composite sheets. I have learned over the years the right formulas and ingredients for putting together a strong head shot and composite sheet. You have to know what will grab the photographer's attention when he, or she, is looking through a stack of composites from an agent for a possible job. For the first couple of years I did everything on pure instinct. Then I realized that I would not progress if I did not study acting.

"You don't have to be beautiful or handsome to be successful. Some people do have a special look that sets them apart and they get hired over and over again. But I look like the guy-next-door. I don't have the kind of look that spins heads as I walk down the street. Having studied acting, I do have the ability to take direction from a photographer or art director and not only give them the look and emotion they want but lots of layers of that look and emotion. My aim at every shoot is to have so many wonderful and different shots that the art director will go crazy struggling to decide which one he will choose. You have to make sure it isn't the other way—a pile of awful shots and he struggles to find one. I can get hired as the nerd, or the dad, or the insurance salesman and everything in between."

Aaron's advice is: "Know what the competition is like and know the dangers in the business. Treat this industry as you would any other kind of business. You wouldn't open up a restaurant without learning about the food industry. Learn how to market yourself. Learn about model release forms, vouchers and everything you can about the business before you jump into it. This knowledge will give you the greatest chance for success."

Aaron put all of this information and much more into his book, "How To Become A Successful Commercial Model." It is excellent and I must add that Aaron's composite is one of the best I have seen.

Personal manager Al Onorato has discovered and developed the careers of many young actors who are household names. His expertise is the theatre, films and television. His workshops and seminars are always packed. Al and his partners, David Guillod and Bobby Moresco own Handprint Entertainment which represents writers, directors, actors, singers and musicians. Al has great charisma. He is admired by everyone and is never too busy to listen and encourage the ingenue–and has always had infinite patience with this persistent author in her quest for information! He has this advice for parents, "Very young children need guidance but not training. Children can get away with a lot because whatever they do is considered cute and charming. They have an innate ability and instincts, which adults tend to push aside. When they are older and start to compete with adults who have had training, they need acting classes. Parents who worry about the expense of drama school should consider local colleges or universities that have drama departments. They usually have someone there with knowledge and it is usually cheaper."

Chapter 14

Plastic Surgery

Dr. Ian Matheson, a plastic surgeon practicing in Tampa, Florida, contributes the following: "Plastic or cosmetic surgery can be a very useful adjunct to a model's career. *Carefully think out the reasons for these surgical changes. Don't be talked into surgery by anyone. A beautiful nose will not ensure a modeling career. Other aspects are involved. Cosmetic surgery must be something you want to have done for you.*

"One reluctant high school senior was brought into my office by her parents, pursuing the parents' idea of modifying her nose and turning her into a model. She did not have the desire, the discipline, or the dedication to be a model. The entire plan was destined to fail. I refused to operate on this girl.

"If you have all the other attributes for a modeling career, but your profile is marred by a nasal hump, or if you have bags under your eyes or a mole that spoils an otherwise clear complexion, corrective surgery could be worthwhile.

"The modeling industry is full of cosmetic surgery success stories. One beautiful blonde had a rounded tip to the end of her nose and examination of her photographs showed a slight shadow cast by the sides of the nose. Surgical corrections resulted in a successful career and her reputation as 'the girl with the perfect features.'

"The camera can be unkind. Even a slight fullness in the lower eyelids (eyebags) is picked up. One model was told by a photographer, 'Your eyelid job has simplified my work - I can now shoot you from any angle.'

"At a modeling convention, a Paris agent told a fledgling model from Florida that her ears protruded. She came to my office and I made the correction. Several years later I saw the same girl, who said, 'The surgery was the best career move I have made. I never think about my ears now.'

"An otherwise beautiful girl with classical features had a birthmark on her right temple. When this was removed it left her with a small scar that could be covered with makeup. She was signed by an American agency and her career was on its way.

"Breast augmentation surgery is both common and successful. It used to be the number-one cosmetic surgical procedure performed in the United States. It has now been replaced by suction lipectomy as the most frequently performed procedure. Suction lipectomy is meant for people who are in basically good shape, but have one or two areas with an abundant accumulation of fat, often hereditary. The most common place for fat removal in women is the thigh and hip area and in men is the 'love handle' and abdomen area. Models, however, must never consider this as a method of weight reduction but must learn to discipline their eating habits.

"Plastic surgery can be a useful tool, but do not have your nose, eyes, ears, breasts, or thighs altered unless it is necessary. Take time before you decide to undergo cosmetic surgery. Be sure that your surgeon is certified by the American Board of Plastic Surgery. Ask your doctor or county medical association to recommend a surgeon. Inquire around the community about his reputation. Ask to see the results of similar types of surgery and talk with other patients of that surgeon. If during the interview you find the surgeon cold, or uncaring, or unwilling to answer all your questions, find a surgeon with whom you feel comfortable. Cosmetic surgery is a serious step. If you do it, do it for yourself. Remember, a perfect profile or features will not guarantee a modeling career. "

Chapter
15

Agency Instructions to New Models

Every well-established agency in the world gives models specific instructions on agency expectations and policy. Models One, in London, is one of the world's top agencies. With their kind permission, I have reprinted a copy of the information they give to their models. It is an excellent example of what it takes to be a professional model. Here it is:

Professionalism:

1. Check-in time is daily between 4:00 P.M. and 5:30 P.M. Don't neglect to call in. If the agency can't get hold of you and you have a job the next day you could be sued if you don't turn up! It's your responsibility to call us each day.

2. When checking in please keep calls brief, as taking up the phone prevents incoming business and that's how we make a living!

3. Keep a pen by the phone with your diary. Always be sure you know all the details of an assignment. ASK! Your date book should also keep track of all payment details. Please also retain your model payment sheets and copies of vouchers to avoid any financial errors. Fill in all the information on your voucher after the booking. Vouchers are due no later than the Friday after the booking or they will not get invoiced in time. They must be signed by the client.

4. Always let the agency know, as far in advance as possible, days or times you are not available so they do not accept any bookings or make any appointments for you.

5. Do not give out your phone number or address, even if it is requested on contracts or application forms. Give the agency's number and/or address.

6. Do not discuss business with the client (rates or other bookings). Pick up the phone and call the agency or have the client call us if there is a question.

7. If (please, NO!) you are going to be late, call the agency, so we can cover for you. If you're late we will find out about it anyway because clients usually like to fill us in on these details! You should be arriving at least fifteen minutes before your booking time to all assignments.

8. Take everything you may ever need to every assignment. Never borrow!

9. A photograph is only as good as the model who's in it. A prepared model is a preferred model. Work your best with each photographer - you should never have to be told every movement. Practice in front of a full-length mirror to understand your body and its best angles.

10. Never apologize for lack of experience, appearance, etc. It only brings it to their attention!

11. Never argue with the client. They pay the bills. Even if you hate the clothes or find their directions foolish, be polite and charming.

12. In this business the most important product people are selling is time, so don't waste anyone's - including your own.

Remember:
On go-sees, remember to take:
a) A-Z (A guidebook of London)
b) Portfolio
c) Extra pictures or card
d) Model's bag (who knows when you'll need it)

What a Model Needs:
-Flesh-colored and black underwear (underpants, waistslip and bras) and a flesh-colored strapless bra.
-Black court shoes [pumps], black evening shoes, plus sporty flat shoes.
-Black or brown boots.
-Good selection of makeup.
-Carmen rollers [hot rollers].
-Selection of tights [hosiery].
-You should also have available and in good condition the following: strappy sandals, jewelry, scarves, sweaters, hats, berets, socks, belts, jeans, cords, etc.

-Your booker will tell you what accessories will be needed for a job. If in doubt-ask.
-When you go to a job you should always have the following with you:
  -Your makeup (even if there is a makeup artist there).
  -Tweezers, scissors, a razor, emery boards, absorbent cotton, cotton wool buds [Q-tips], nail varnish remover, tissues, cleanser, toner, moisturizer.
  -Brush, comb, hairgrips [bobby pins] and Carmen rollers.
  -Flesh-colored underwear.
  -A large scarf.
  -A folded umbrella.
  -A-Z of London.

Remember:
1. Hands to be well manicured at all times.
2. Feet to be frequently pedicured.
3. Legs and underarms to be shaved or waxed regularly.
4. Clean, neat hair.

Chapter 16

What to Pack

My husband questions my qualifications as an expert in the field of packing. He constantly reminds me of one particular train trip through Europe, on which he had to rent an additional sleeping compartment for our luggage alone. Suffice it to say, "Do as I say, not as I do." Extra baggage is costly and burdensome, especially in Europe, where models move from country to country on assignments. When packing, take into consideration the season and climate of the country where you will work. However, if you are going to be there in winter, remember, you will be modeling spring and summer fashions and therefore you should pack appropriate accessories.

In addition to your basic wardrobe, here are additional items you should pack: a dual-voltage hair dryer and rollers; a voltage converter kit (this contains plugs for virtually all international outlets and an adapter that handles appliances up to 1600 watts); a foreign-language cassette and tape recorder; a cordless battery-operated hair comb or curler; an alarm clock (preferably one that doesn't tick-if you don't object to the tick at night, your roommate might); camera and film; a sewing kit; scissors (pack these in your main luggage-they might not pass security inspection of hand luggage on international flights); safety pins; umbrella; slippers (European floors are often tiled and therefore cold); miniature clothesline and pins; pocket calculator; address book and an appointment book.

It is important to carry passport, visa, tickets, travelers checks and the address and telephone number of your foreign agency in a pocketbook or man's jacket. These items must never be in checked luggage. Make sure you have strong locks for your luggage. It is a good idea to buy a model's bag before you go abroad and you can use this to carry hand luggage.

Listed below are items that should always be in your model's bag and taken on assignments.

-Makeup remover
-Skin toner
-Light foundation (1 shade darker than your skin tone)
- Dark foundation (3 shades darker than your skin tone)
-Loose powder with puff
-Compact powder
-Eyebrow pencils (+ sharpener)
-Lip brushes and eyeliner brushes
-Big soft brushes (for blush)
-Eyebrow brush
-Tweezers
-Blush
-Eye shadows
-Cover stick
-Different lipsticks-all colors, including natural gloss
-Mascara
-Eyeliner
-Nail polishes (3 or 4 different tints)
-Nail polish remover (pack polish and remover in leak proof bag)
-Little sponges (for foundation)
-Nail file or emery board
-Brush and comb
-Mirror
-Hair accessories and curling iron, or hot rollers

Obviously all these products and accessories must be in good condition and you must renew them whenever necessary so that your kit is always complete. Certain articles of clothing are essential:
-Different panty hose.
-Lingerie (brassieres and panties), flesh color.

Chapter

17

Helpful Information

Take time out before departure to learn the metric system, the twentyfour-hour clock, foreign clothing and shoe sizes and other important terms. The more you can learn before you go the less traumatic the culture shock will be. This information is necessary for travel overseas.

Metric System

1 mile = 1.609 kilometers (km)	1 kilometer = 0.621 miles
1 yard = 0.914 meters (m)	1 meter = 1.094 yards
1 foot = 0.305 meters (m)	1 meter = 3.281 feet
1 inch = 2.54 centimeters (cm)	1 centimeter = 0.39 inches
1 pound = 0.453 kilograms(kg)	1 kilogram = 2.205 pounds
1 U.S. gallon = 3.785 liters (L)	1 liter = 0.264 U.S. gallons
1 imperial gallon = 4.545 liters	1 liter = 0.22 imperial gallons

Twenty-Four Hour Clock

In the twenty-four-hour clock, each hour is referred to in hundreds, i.e. 1:00 A.M., is referred to as 0100 hours. As in the normal clock, the morning hours are 1-12; the afternoon hours are referred to as 1300 (thirteen hundred) hours to 2400 (twenty-four hundred) hours. Thus, 1:00 p.m. is 1300 hours. If you are given a time greater than 12:00 noon you have only to subtract 1200 in order to establish what that time would be, e.g. 1800 hours is 1800 - 1200 = 6:00 p.m. Practice this and you will find it easy to learn in either the standard or twenty-four-hour clock. The latter removes the ambiguity of A.M. and P.M.

Greenwich Mean Time (GMT)

You will hear this term in your travels. Greenwich (pronounced "Grennich") Mean Time is the standard time in Britain and the means by which standard time is measured around the world. Time in other countries is referred to as being behind (earlier than) GMT or ahead of (later than) GMT.

Temperature

To change Fahrenheit into centigrade subtract 32 from Fahrenheit and divide by 1.8. To convert centigrade into Fahrenheit, multiply centigrade by 1.8 and add 32.

International Telephone Direct Dialing

Direct dialing is not possible between all countries. To dial direct, you will need the international access code of the country you are in, plus the country code, plus the city code, plus the number. For example, to call Milan from the United States, you would dial 0 11 (international access code for the United States) plus 39 (country code for Italy) plus 02 (city code for Milan) plus number.

International Clothing Sizes *(Continental sizes are approximate)*

Women's Dresses

American	6	8	10
British	8	10	12
Continental	34/36	36/38	38/40
France and Spain	36/38	38/40	40/42
Italy	40	42	44
Australian	6	8	10

Women's Shoes

American	7	8	9
British	5¹/₂	6¹/₂	7¹/₂
Continental	38	40	41
Japanese	9.7	10.3	10.7

Hosiery

American	8	8¹/₂	9	10
British	8	8¹/₂	9	10
Continental	0	1	2	4

Men's Suits and Coats

American	36	38	42
British	36	38	42
Continental	46	48	52
Australian	92	97	102

Shirts

American	14	14¹/₂	15	15¹/₂	16
British	14	14¹/₂	15	15¹/₂	16
Continental	36	37	38	39	41
Australian	36	37	38	39	40

Men's Shoes

American	8	8¹/₂	9	10	11
British	7¹/₂	8	8¹/₂	9¹/₂	10¹/₂
Continental	42	43	43	44	45

Models Mart

Models Mart, at 42 West 38th Street, Suite 802, New York, NY, 10018, is the international connection for models, actors, agents and school directors. They customize portfolios for agencies and models as well as sell books, directories, video tapes and other material which help models and actors improve their talent.

The authority at Models Mart is David Vando, a playwright, lyricist, author and actor. He became the owner of Models Mart by accident. He had taken a leave of absence from the Metropolitan Opera Company in New York to produce a play in Washington. This project finished and with the Opera Company on summer hiatus, David responded to a friend's call to help with research for the Peter Glenn Publishing Company. His plans to return to the Met in the Fall changed again when the Opera Company went on strike for six months. He was asked to continue working with the publishing firm which had an adjunct company called Models Mart. Ultimately David became the owner. He told me: "As so often happens in the theatre, one person auditions for a part and doesn't get it. Another person who doesn't know anything about the audition walks in and they say 'You are the one.' There is a certain luck and happenstance that is beyond our control."

In 1994, David was inducted into the Models Hall of Fame (the first inductee was the late, great Wilhelmina) which honors those who have striven for excellence in serving the modeling profession. He has been an advisor and friend to many people in the industry all over the world—including me. Here is David's advice to aspiring models: "Read, ask questions and learn everything you can about the industry. The more you know the better prepared you will be physically and mentally. You will be in a stronger position not to be taken advantage of by people who will trade on your aspirations. Anyone pursuing the performing arts, especially in the United States, must be prepared to support themselves in areas that may not directly relate to their art. Then they can support their dreams and be happy."

The number for Models Mart is 212-944-0638

Peter Glenn Publications

Years ago a successful and enterprising model by the name of Peter Glenn compiled a resource list of clients, photographers, stylists and others in the industry whom he met while traveling throughout the world as a model and a scholar. The list continued to grow until 1956 when Peter Glenn Publications published the first MADISON AVENUE HANDBOOK. Today, Gregory James, his wife, Tricia and Peter's successor, Chip Brill own the company. Peter Glenn Publications is recognized as the leading authority on information about the entertainment industry. They publish several resource directories for film, music, fashion, modeling and acting. Their INTERNATIONAL DIRECTORY OF MODEL & TALENT AGENCIES & SCHOOLS is a universally recognized and highly-respected compilation of all the reputable model and talent agencies and schools in the world. It also includes information on legitimate modeling conventions, searches and competitions. Virtually everyone interviewed for THE MODELING HANDBOOK is listed in the Directory, which lists addresses, phone and fax numbers and other important information.

Greg is a good example of a successful model who went through college and explored all of his options before finding what was right for him. He studied film production and fashion photography at the University of South Carolina. For extra money, Greg decided to do modeling on the weekends. "I did a modeling course and later became an instructor at the school. I went to a modeling convention and was accepted with the Zoli agency in New York." Once Greg received his degree in film production, he worked on several major motion pictures. He also was exposed to the publishing business around this time. As Greg became more involved in publishing, all three careers became too demanding. He finally made the decision to focus solely on publishing. Greg said, "I found I loved this business. I had paid my dues as a model and understood the industry. I also appreciated what Peter Glenn began and wanted to keep up the tradition of providing valuable information for the entertainment industry."

Peter Glenn Publications is located at 42 West 38th Street, Suite 802, New York, New York 10018. Telephone: (212) 869-2020. Toll Free: (888) 332-6700. Fax: (212) 354-4099. Or visit their web site: www.peterglennpublications.com

The Models Guild

The Models Guild, a union which protects models and other professionals associated with the modeling industry, was founded by Amy Bongay in New York in November, 1995. Soon after, Donna Eller became president. Rhonda Hudson took over as president of the union in March, 1999. A model and aspiring actress herself, she hopes that The Models Guild can do for models what the Screen Actors Guild does for actors.

Hudson has several issues she would like to tackle as president of the union. One problem is that designers are using fourteen-year old models on the runway. Certainly a fourteen-year old can't afford a $650 gown! Other issues include drug abuse, sexual abuse, eating disorders and race discrimination. Some models are upset that they have been losing magazine covers to celebrities. While Hudson understands the appeal of celebrities, she also acknowledges that models are mostly anonymous.

On the other hand, Rhonda is happy to see some changes in the modeling industry. She is happy the heroin-chic and waif looks are out. "It is one thing to be skinny, and it is entirely different to be sick," Rhonda said.

The Models Guild provides a number of services including health insurance, legal services and loans, among other things. Already the union has helped recover money lost in unpaid fees and money scams. The union does most of its work in Los Angeles and New York, but is also working in Florida to pass legislation on the modeling industry. Models are encouraged to contact The Models Guild to air grievances and be informed about many career-related issues. Keep an eye out for a new web site Rhonda plans to launch, with public service announcements for anyone interested in a modeling career.

To join The Models Guild, the models must have at least two modeling jobs in the year they join. There is also an annual membership fee of $300. For non-models who work with models, such as stylists and make-up artists, the nonvoting membership fee is $165 per year.

For more information about the union, contact: The Models Guild, Local 51, Office and Professional Employees International

Union (OPEIU), AFL-CIO, 265 W. 14th Street, Suite 203, N.Y. N.Y. 10011. Tel. (800) 864-4696; New York residents, (212) 675-4133; Fax: (212) 675-3066.

Chapter

18

Competitions, Conventions and Model Searches

Model and talent competitions, model searches and conventions are excellent ways to learn about the business, be discovered and to find out if modeling and/or acting is the career for you. There is controversy over the value and validity of these events. Some are organized brilliantly and offer unquestionable value.

How can you evaluate a convention and how can you benefit from attending? Conventions afford young men and women the opportunity to discuss career potential and ambitions with experts in the industry. The purpose of these events is to bring together models and talent from all over the country, casting directors from Los Angeles and New York and model agents from all over the world. Conventions vary in format but generally include competitions, workshops, seminars, callbacks, open interviews and panel discussions. A well-run convention is beneficial to all concerned. Benefits include: contracts, trophies, advice from professionals and deep insight into what is required in the modeling and acting professions. Parents have the opportunity to learn about the business. Agents and casting directors have a chance to scout for models and talent and to exchange ideas with colleagues.

If you plan to attend a convention, you must be assured that reputable agents will be present and that a specific time will be set aside for you to meet them. This is usually done during call backs (the allotted time for agents to see models or talent in whom they have expressed a specific interest), or open interviews (another opportunity for all participants to see the agents of their choice). I must point out, however, that sometimes at the last minute, a celebrity may become ill, a casting director may cancel because a casting has run much longer than expected or he or she has business requiring immediate attention. A model agent may bow out because of sudden staff problems or the arrival of an out-of-town client. I have seen this happen on occasion. Unavoidable cancellations are understandable, but they can cause embarrassment and shake the credibility of the convention producer in the eyes of the school directors, students, parents and other agents. Be aware that this can happen and try to understand. By the same token convention planners would do well to drop an agent, casting director, or celebrity who makes a last-minute cancellation on two or more occasions.

A convention is not only a great opportunity to have fun, meet a lot of people, gain experience and learn the business, it is also a launching pad for many careers. Models and actors are usually brought to these events by directors of modeling schools, promoters of model search events, or advertisements in the media. Some form of specialized preparation is advisable before participating in a convention. This can be obtained from most modeling schools.

Now let us discuss the financial aspect. There will be a registration fee and possible additional fees for competitions and workshops. Usually, the investment is worthwhile. You will meet the experts of the industry from all over the world, at one location, over the period of the convention (approximately 3-5 days). The alternative to attending a convention would involve traveling to New York, Chicago, Dallas, Los Angeles, Miami and foreign cities at great expense, without any guarantee that you would meet your chosen agency representatives. I can assure you that when convention planners are establishing fees, choosing hotels and planning menus, the restricted budgets of the young people they hope to attract greatly influence their final decisions. I can also assure you that the cost of putting on a convention is great. The planning takes at least a year. Expenses include: travel and accommodation for agents and casting directors, lawyers' fees, a convention staff, security, a highly specialized technical crew, camera and video equipment, a stage production to showcase participating talent and many other necessities.

I would suggest that you study the program of events well in advance with your school director. First-time participation at a convention can be an overwhelming experience. While the staff will be prepared to answer questions, the demands on their time are great. I have attended many conventions. A behind-the-scenes glimpse of my experiences will give you some idea of the problems the staff is expected to handle. There was the mother in the elevator who appeared to be having a heart attack but was in fact hyperventilating because her child did not win a competition! I remember the contestant who fell and, in true show business fashion, insisted on finishing her act. Later it was discovered she had broken her leg. In the same vein, there was the school director who was rushed to hospital for an appendectomy only to return the next night complete with stitches, nurse and doctor to see her school sweep to victory at an awards banquet. At the end of another convention I met one puzzled foreign agent who had missed the entire event by spending his stay at the wrong hotel—models are not the only people confused by a language barrier and a new location!

I asked some well-known personalities who have attended conventions for their views on these events. Mrs. Muriel Alt, who attended a convention with her daughter, top model Carol Alt, said: "I am amazed at the caliber of people who are here and at how accessible they are to the boys and girls. At a convention like this young people can learn how much hard work is involved in the profession. They may also realize that acting and modeling is not for them. I feel only good can come out of this event." Carol told contestants: "You are very fortunate to have what this convention offers. Take advantage of the workshops. Get advice from the experts here."

Allen Fawcett, who co-authored the book *Kid Biz* said: "A convention is a means to an end. It is one step in a series of steps that must be taken in the pursuit of a career. It is about shopping your wares and about learning. If you are going to make mistakes, make them at a convention, not in the marketplace. If you have shortcomings, discover what they are before you go any further. Show business is a devastating profession for someone who has had a commodity called 'false hope' packaged and sold to them. A convention can be a valuable service if it is planned under controlled conditions."

Tony Shepherd of Aaron Spelling Productions said: "The competition is almost secondary to the benefits that the artists receive. These young people—I prefer to call them artists—have the opportunity to acquire a great deal of knowledge."

The International Modeling and Talent Association (IMTA), which is headquartered in Phoenix, Arizona, holds its annual convention, in Los Angeles in January and in New York in July. It is the industry standard by which other conventions can be judged. President Helen Rogers, her daughter Pamela Edwards and Nancy Mancuso are the masterminds behind this marathon of workshops, seminars and competitions. They are helped by Cameron Vessey (Helen's granddaughter) and a large, delightful staff. Participants are brought to the convention by school directors. Both students and directors have access to the world's most notable casting directors and model agents. These experts judge contestants, discuss possible contracts during callbacks and offer career guidance during open interviews.

School directors soak up information from panels, seminars and workshops given by industry experts and Helen Rogers herself.

Helen, a former Ford model, told me: "After a modeling career in New York and Los Angeles, I opened a modeling school—Plaza 3 in Phoenix, Arizona. We made is as professional as it could possibly be. We had a tiny agency but we ran it like a New York agency. We had a very good reputation because we were honest.

"Plaza 3 became the largest-grossing school with the largest student enrollment in the country. We were accredited by the National Association of Trade and Technical Schools and we introduced fashion merchandising, interior design and commercial photography. Our modeling program was also accredited. Because of this accreditation we were able to obtain federal grant and loan programs. It also meant we had to have a placement office and a student guidance center.

"I was the most successful school director in the country and I made all the mistakes in the book. I don't want other school directors to make the same mistakes. I did lots of good things too. I want to share all of this with school owners and directors and encourage them to update their curriculum. As members of our organization they have the opportunity to have their students discovered by international agents. When an agent realizes that a school turns out good models, that school often becomes a recruitment source. There is no mystique about this. This is how it can and should work."

Pamela Edwards, senior vice president of IMTA, said: "This organization works because we are totally committed to making IMTA the best educational experience for the school directors and the talent. We are known internationally as the best discovery source for models and actors available anywhere. We listen to the input of everyone involved and implement suggestions wherever we can."

The list of IMTA's successes is truly amazing. They include: top international models Beverly Peele, Christina Thé and Sara Dawson; male model Joel West who signed a $1,000,000 contract with Calvin Klein; child star Elijah Wood who appeared with Katie Holmes (another IMTA discovery) in the Cannes Film Festival opener Ice Storm and Jeremy Kissner who starred in Great Expectations with Robert DeNiro and Gwyneth Paltrow. There are many others. I spoke to several industry experts who attend this convention on a regular basis. Here is what they said. Clair Sinnett (Clair Sinnett Casting, Bel Air, CA): "It would take an actor years to meet the industry professionals he or she can meet in one week, under one roof, here at the IMTA convention. I wish I had had this opportunity when I was starting my career."

Al Onorato (Handprint Entertainment), a personal manager who has made several very successful discoveries at this convention, commented: "It provides an enormous link between people in the business and people who cannot just pick up and go to one of the major markets such as Los Angeles, New York, Chicago, or Europe. It gives me a chance to see untrained talent that may have some potential. It also gives me a chance to encourage them in that area or perhaps encourage them to explore other areas."

Adam Hill (artist-in-residence, Wilkes University): "Integrity, talent, class, respect and hard work permeate the entire convention."

Beatrice Traissac of International Beatrice Models in Milan: "This is a very serious convention. I have seen beautiful girls here and will be taking some to Milan."

Judy La Grone (school director and talent scout): "IMTA is an unbeatable education for anyone who wants to be in the business." Actress Faith Ford who became famous for her role in MURPHY BROWN was a student of Judy's some years ago. At an awards banquet where she presented a scholarship in her name, she told contestants:

"You may not win every award and you may not get the job after every audition, but the true test of really wanting to be an actor is the determination to improve your skills. IMTA is a fabulous experience. This scholarship makes me feel very grateful." The Faith Ford Award, which is a $1000 scholarship, is presented to a student who has demonstrated a particular talent and has potential for success. The money is used to further the student's career.

Here is an example of another opportunity to be discovered. It has a different approach and does not involve competitions, seminars or awards. It is strictly an opportunity for top agents to meet potential models. Brian Marcus, who was a model agent for eight years, holds what he calls a "Two-Day Meet The Agent Invitational". This is organized by his Chicago-based company, Pro-Scout, Inc. Over twelve of these weekend events are held in various parts of the United States and Canada each year. Credibility and integrity are the basic philosophy which, combined with economy, spell success for Pro-Scout and participants. Explaining his concept, Brian told me: "We scout and prescreen applicants with potential talent. Top agents are then flown into a central location to meet them. The entire weekend is designed to be efficient for agents and cost effective for models and parents."

Brian is very concerned about the increasing number of scams. He said: "People who don't have potential should be told that before their parents mortgage their homes to spend money on events that will lead nowhere. There are conventions and model searches that are respected by the top agencies and others that are pathetic scams. Judge them by their performance. Can the organizers verify which of the top agencies in the world will be represented. Whom have they discovered in the last six months, as opposed to ten years ago? Trust your instincts. Ask questions and see if they can answer them without making false promises. The people I trust in the business are the people who will tell me the pitfalls to avoid. Calling the Better Business Bureau for verification is not the answer. I hate to say this, because I am a member, but all they can tell you is if somebody has a bad record. They can't give you any information about the quality and expertise of the people involved. The success of Pro-Scout is based on the high caliber of agents we bring in and the number of people discovered who are working worldwide as a result of what we do."

David Mogull, a former Ford model, attended many modeling

conventions as an agent before starting Model Search America in January, 1993. He told me: "I would go to conventions and wonder if anyone really understood the dream those young contestants had. I could feel their fears. I could understand their passion. I wanted to help them. I wanted to make a difference in their lives." I was impressed and moved by his concern for all contestants. To David, launching successful careers is important, but equally as important is the time he spends encouraging, consoling and advising the less successful participants.

David's background made him aware that aspiring models had a difficult time finding legitimate agencies and that agencies had a difficult and expensive time scouting for new models. His Model Search America provides an excellent service for everyone. Sixteen regional review conventions, basically model searches, are held annually in major cities in the United States. Experts screen aspiring models in advance during personal interviews. Successful applicants are invited to attend one of the regional events where they are interviewed by top model, commercial print, and television casting agencies. Vice President Peter Buttenweiser told me: "We bring in agents from all over the United States, Europe and Asia. Our events are time efficient and save everyone money." Peter's advice to parents and potential models is: "As in any business, some investment has to be made if you are to progress. But be smart! If something seems too good to be true, then it is. The business is about hard work, perseverance and commitment."

The Elite Model Look is the world's largest model search and has an impressive track record. The majority of finalists enjoy successful modeling careers withing two years of the event. It is organized by the world famous Elite agency to find and develop new talent. Snapshots are all that are required to enter. The search starts in January each year and culminates in a spectacular international finale in Europe.

Here is a partial list of people who have had successful conventions, competitions and model searches. They are listed in alphabetical order. Addresses, telephone numbers and contacts, for these and other events are listed in the INTERNATIONAL DIRECTORY OF MODEL AND TALENT AGENCIES AND SCHOOLS (Peter Glenn Publications. Tel: (212) 869-2020, (888) 332-6700).

Carey Lewis Arban and her husband Dr. Bill Arban are the founders and owners of the Millie Lewis American Modeling and Talent

Convention which is held in Orlando in July and on Hilton Head Island in January. It is renowned for the calibre and number of agents and casting directors who attend and for the success rate of its participants. Carey's mother, Millie Lewis, a beautiful former New York model, owned a chain of respected, successful modeling schools in South Carolina and Georgia for many years. Carey told me: "I was raised in the modeling business and my mom is definitely our role model. Our focus is on education, not only for the potential model, but for the whole family." Her advice to aspiring models is: "Go to the library and read every good book on the modeling industry. Try to get your feet wet locally with a reputable school or agency. Find out if you have an aptitude for this business. Take it one step at a time. Don't go jetting off to New York with high hopes and no knowledge."

Mike Beaty of Dallas, is a charming, charismatic man with excellent contacts worldwide. Mike is a former model and highly respected in the business. The MB Model and Talent Expo offers workshops, seminars, competitions, awards, callbacks and the opportunity to meet and perform for the world's top modeling and talent agents, personal managers, casting directors and industry experts. Three model and talent expos and an actors/talent/ singers expo are held annually. Southern warmth and hospitality prevail at all events. Informality and efficiency make this a comfortable, rewarding experience for everyone.

The Canadian Model and Talent Convention is endorsed by the world's top modeling and talent agents. This is a full-scale, well run event which offers workshops, seminars, competitions, awards and callbacks.

The Modeling Association of America International has a long history of integrity. It provides another excellent opportunity for models, actors, singers and dancers to be seen, judged and discovered by experts in the industry. The convention is held annually at the beautiful Waldorf Astoria in New York.

R. Jack Rasnic is a true industry pioneer who holds the Models of the South convention at Hilton Head, South Carolina, the weekend before Thanksgiving every year.

Ford Models Inc. has its famous "Supermodel of the World" event and Elite Models presents the renowned "Look of the Year" contest.

In conclusion, anyone who is interested in a modeling career and who has had little or no exposure to the business would be advised to attend a convention or model search. I stated at the beginning of this chapter that competitions, conventions and searches come and go. I advise you to check credentials before making any financial commitment. When you are satisfied, go to the event, throw yourself into it, learn what you can and enjoy a once-in-a-lifetime experience.

•••••

This book is based on the knowledge and advice from people who have been in the modeling business for many years. Sound basic principles and good advice never date.

Please remember that the only true failure is never having tried. Don't be afraid to try! What you can accomplish with the raw materials God has given you is up to you. Good luck with your career.

Personal Phone Pages

Name & Address	Phone/Fax

Name & Address	Phone/Fax

Other titles from
Peter Glenn Publications

The International Directory of Model & Talent
  Agencies & Schools

The Image Makers Source

The Production Makers Source

The National Casting Guide

The New York City Model Agency Directory

The Miami Model Agency Directory

Model-The Complete Guide for Men & Women